the 365 DAY Clean Joke Book

the 365 DAY

Clean Joke

Book

Three Laughers
A Day for every
day of the year!

BARBOUR
PUBLISHING

© 2006 by Barbour Publishing, Inc.

Compiled by Connie Troyer.

ISBN 978-1-59789-650-4

Material previously published in *Noah's Favorite Animal Jokes*; *The World's Greatest Collection of Church Jokes*; *The Good Sports Joke Book*; *The Teacher, Teacher Joke Book*; *Knock-Knock, Who's There?*; *Lots o' Riddles*; *The Ultimate Joke Book*; *The Joke's on Ewe*; *777 Great Clean Jokes*; *Clean Jokes for Kids*; *The Book of Clean Jokes*; *Great Clean Jokes for Kids*; *Great Clean Jokes for Grown-Up Kids*; and *More Clean Jokes for Kids*.

Published by Barbour Publishing, P.O. Box 719, Uhrichsville, Ohio 44683, www.barbourbooks.com

Our mission is to publish and distribute inspirational products offering exceptional value and biblical encouragement to the masses.

Member of the
Evangelical Christian
Publishers Association

Printed in the United States of America.

INTRODUCTION

How does one angel greet another?
She says, "Halo!"

A father was showing pictures of his wedding day to his son.
"Is that when Mommy came to work for us?" the boy asked.

Knock-knock.
Who's there?
Lettuce.
Lettuce who?
Lettuce pray.

Tickle your funny bone with *The 365-Day Clean Joke Book*! Every day for an entire year, you'll find three great jokes, from the hilarious to some real groaners, on a wide variety of topics—church and children, sports and school, marriage, music, and the military. And that's not all! If you order now—oops, wrong line—you'll also find jokes on travel, crime, food, animals, and just about everything else under the sun. Funny quotes, bloopers, riddles, and knock-knocks round out the collection, promising an assortment of smiles, chuckles, snickers, chortles, and whoops.

According to the Bible's book of Proverbs, "A merry heart doeth good like a medicine." Give your heart a daily dose of healthy humor, and exercise your laughter reflex. Who knows? *The 365-Day Clean Joke Book* might just change your life!

Little Johnny was bothered with a question that he had to ask his Sunday school teacher. "Miss Davis, are there any animals in heaven?"

"I'm not sure, Johnny," his teacher responded.

"Well, I just wanted to know, 'cause last Sunday we sang about 'Gladly the Cross-Eyed Bear.'"

⊙⊙⊙

Definitions given by children in a Sunday school class:

Conversion: "The point after a touchdown."
Fast Days: "The days you have to eat in a hurry."
Epistle: "The wife of an apostle."

⊙⊙⊙

A young husband and wife invited their pastor for Sunday dinner. While they were in the kitchen preparing the meal, their young son was in the living room entertaining the pastor.

"What are we having for dinner?" the minister asked.

"Goat," replied the boy.

"Goat?" repeated the startled pastor. "Are you sure about that?"

"Yep," said the youngster. "I heard Dad tell Mom, 'Might as well have the old goat for dinner today as any other day.'"

Frank: "Did you hear about the guy who was arrested at the zoo for feeding the pigeons?"

Harry: "No. What's wrong with feeding the pigeons?"

Frank: "He fed them to the lions."

What did the teddy bear say when he was offered dessert? *"No thanks, I'm stuffed."*

It was a boring afternoon in the jungle, so the elephants decided to challenge the ants to a game of soccer. The game was going well, with the elephants beating the mighty ants ten goals to zip, when the ants gained possession.

The ants' star player was advancing the ball toward the elephants' goal when the elephants' leftback came lumbering toward him. The elephant trod on the little ant, killing him instantly.

The referee stopped the game. "What do you think you're doing? Do you call that sportsmanship, killing another player?"

The elephant sadly replied, "I didn't mean to kill him—I was just trying to trip him up."

It was Johnny Carson who asked this thought-provoking question: "If airline travel is so safe, how come flight attendants sit right next to the emergency exit?"

⊙⊙⊚

"Golf is *flog* spelled backwards." —Bob Hope

⊚⊙⊚

Grandpop: "Lincoln was right when he said, 'You can fool all the people some of the time and some of the people all the time.'"

Grandson: "But what happens the rest of the time?"

Grandpop: "They're likely to make fools of themselves, I reckon."

Why wasn't Cinderella good at sports?
Because she had a pumpkin as her coach!

◉◉◉

A tribal chieftain returned to his native country after a visit to the United States. "The Americans," he reported to his people, "have greater magic than us."

"Can they make it rain?" asked a tribeswoman.

"Whenever they want."

"How?"

"They gather thousands of people around a flat, green meadow. Warriors blowing horns and beating drums line up at each end of the meadow and make strange music. Then women wearing few clothes and shaking little clumps of grass run between the warriors onto the meadow, pursued by other warriors wearing colorful, shiny headdresses. They do this at both ends of the meadow. Then the two groups of warriors wearing funny headdresses at both ends of the meadow form themselves into lines facing each other. One group of warriors kicks a brown ball to the other group, and they all clash and fight for the ball. *And then it begins to rain.*"

◉◉◉

Bob: "You know what your main golf problem is?"

Ted: "What?"

Bob: "You stand too close to the ball after you've hit it."

Day
4

I am the ruler of shovels.
I have a double.
I am as thin as a knife.
I have a wife.
What am I?
The King of Spades (from a deck of cards).

⊙⊙⊙

What color hair did the Wicked Witch of the West have?
Brewnette.

⊙⊙⊙

An archeologist found a coin dated 62 BC and immediately declared it a fraud. How did he know it wasn't real?
BC *stands for "Before Christ." This dating system wasn't used until after Christ had been born.*

Little Tony was in his uncle's wedding. As he came down the aisle during the ceremony, he carefully took two steps, then stopped and turned to the crowd. When facing the congregation he put his hands up like claws and roared loudly. So it went, step, step, turn, *roar*, step, step, turn, *roar*, all the way down the aisle.

As you can imagine, the congregation was near tears from laughing. By the time little Tony reached the altar, he was near tears, too. When later asked what he was doing, the boy sniffed and said, "I was being the Ring Bear."

◉◉◉

"Mommy, Randall just broke the bedroom window!"
"Oh, no! How did that happen?"
"I threw a shoe at him, and he ducked."

◉◉◉

Jon: "My parents just got a new computer for my teenaged sister."
Ron: "I wish my parents could make that kind of trade for *my* big sister."

Ole got a new cell phone, and on his way home on the freeway, he called his wife, Lena.

"Hello, Lena. I'm calling you from the freeway on my new cell phone."

Lena says, "Be careful, Ole. The radio says that some nut is driving the wrong way on the freeway."

Ole says, "One nut, my eye. There are hundreds of them!"

◉ ⊙ ◎

Definitions:

Low Mileage: What you get when your car won't start.
Steering Committee: A panel of individuals who aren't capable of driving by themselves.

◉ ⊙ ◎

One day a father was driving with his five-year-old daughter, when he honked his car horn by mistake.

"I did that by accident," he said.

"I know that, Daddy," she replied.

"How did you know that?"

"Because you didn't holler at the other driver after you honked it."

Patient: "Doctor, sometimes when I wake up in the morning I think I'm Donald Duck; other times I think I'm Mickey Mouse."

Doctor: "How long have you had these Disney spells?"

◉◉◉

A young man brought his wife to a small-town doctor's office in an emergency. The nurses escorted the woman to the examination area, and the husband anxiously took a seat in the lobby.

For the next few minutes, he could hear the doctor bark an unsettling string of orders to the staff. First it was "Screwdriver!" Then "Knife!" Then "Pliers!"

When he heard "Sledgehammer!" the young man could bear the tension no longer. He burst into the examination room and shrieked, "Doctor, what's *wrong* with her?"

"We have no idea," the doctor said. "Right now, we're still trying to open the medicine cabinet."

◉◉◉

A pharmacist was squinting and holding the prescription slip up to the light. Finally, she took up a magnifier in a futile effort to read it.

"We don't think too highly of this particular doctor," she told the customer, "but there's one thing he obviously can do better than anyone else on the planet."

"What's that?"

"Read his own handwriting!"

Day
8

A senior class had behaved abominably at an assembly program, and at the end the school principal announced sternly that there would be no outdoor recess for seniors for the remainder of the week.

As he turned from the podium, from the middle of the crowded assembly hall came a shout: "Give me liberty, or give me death!"

"Who said that?" demanded the principal, wheeling about.

There was a short silence. Then another anonymous voice called out, "Patrick Henry?"

⊙⊙⊙

How did the colonists react to the sugar tax?
They raised cane.

⊙⊙⊙

Teacher: "Can anyone tell me why the Capitol in Washington has a rotunda?"
Student: "So our politicians can run around in circles."

Where did Sherlock Holmes go to school?
Elementary, dear Watson.

◉ ⊙ ◎

Teacher: "If you had one dollar and you asked your father for
  another, how many dollars would you have?"
Boy: "One dollar."
Teacher: "Sorry, you don't know your arithmetic."
Boy: "You don't know my father."

◉ ⊙ ◎

An ironworker nonchalantly walked the narrow beam fifteen
floors above the city sidewalk. Even though a hurricane was
blowing and heavy rain was falling, the worker exhibited no
fear and was foot-perfect.

When he came down to the sidewalk, a man who had been
watching him from ground level went over to him and said, "I
was really impressed watching you up there. You were so calm.
How did you get a job like this?"

"Well, as a matter of fact," replied the ironworker, "I used to
drive a school bus, until my nerves gave out."

Knock-knock.
Who's there?
Irish Stew.
Irish Stew who?
Irish stew would stay for dinner.

⊙⊙⊙

Knock-knock.
Who's there?
Ben Hur.
Ben Hur who?
Ben Hur an hour an' she ain't in sight.

⊙⊙⊙

Knock-knock.
Who's there?
Safari.
Safari who?
Safari, so good.

What did Noah do for a living?
He was an ark-itect.

◉◉◉

When a traffic cop pulled over Pastor Johnson for speeding, the minister reminded the officer, "Blessed are the merciful, for they shall obtain mercy."

The cop handed the minister the ticket and quoted, "Go thou and sin no more."

◉◉◉

Adam and Eve had the perfect marriage. He didn't have to listen to her talk about men she knew before him, and she didn't have to put up with his mother.

Boy: "Could you sell me a shark?"
Pet shop owner: "Why do you want a shark?"
Boy: "My cat keeps trying to eat my goldfish, and I want to
    teach him a lesson."

⊙⊙⊙

A police dog responds to an ad for work with the FBI. "Well,"
says the personnel director, "you'll have to meet some strict
requirements. First, you must type at least sixty words per
minute."

Sitting at the typewriter, the dog types out eighty words
per minute.

"Also," says the director, "you must pass a physical exam
and complete the obstacle course."

This perfect canine finished the course in record time.

"There's one last requirement," the director continues,
"you must be bilingual."

With confidence, the dog looks up at him and says,
"Meow!"

⊙⊙⊙

Why did Mozart sell his chickens?
They kept saying, "Bach, Bach, Bach."

Bulletin Blooper: "Ushers will swat latecomers at these points in the service."

☉⊙◎

Necessity is the mother of invention—even though much of what's invented is hardly necessary.

☉⊙◎

A lady sent the following letter to a mail-order house: "Gentlemen: Please send me the frying pan on page 10 of your catalog. If it's any good, I'll send you $14.95 by return mail."

The reply came back: "Madam: Please send us your check for $14.95. If it's any good, we'll send you the frying pan by return mail."

An angler looked up from the stream and spoke to the man sitting above him on the bank: "You've been sitting there watching me fish for two hours now. Why don't you just fish yourself?"

"Ain't got the patience for it."

⦿⦿⦿

It was sportscaster Howard Cossell who defined *sports* as "the toy department of human life."

⦿⦿⦿

"I like the statistics of your quarterback, Evans," a pro scout told a college football coach. "What's your opinion of him personally?"

"Good skills. Sort of a *prima donna*, though."

"How do you mean?"

"Well, let's just say when he makes a big play, he's a big advocate of the idea of taking personal responsibility for the way things happen. When he gets sacked, he's a big advocate of the concept of luck."

In what country can fish survive out of water?
Finland.

⊙⊙⊚

A boat has a ladder that has six rungs. Each rung is one foot apart. The bottom rung is one foot from the water. The tide rises at twelve inches every fifteen minutes. High tide peaks in one hour. When the tide is at its highest, how many rungs are under water?
None. The boat rises with the tide.

⊙⊙⊚

What can you always find to eat if you're shipwrecked on a desert island?
Lots of SAND-wiches.

"Mom, I want a pet skunk," said Tricia.

"And where, exactly, do you propose to keep it?"

"In my brother's room."

"What would he do about the terrible odor?"

"I'm sure the skunk's used to it."

⊙⊙⊙

Who's married to Antarctica?

Uncle Arctica.

⊙⊙⊙

A young child walked up to her mother and stared at her hair. As her mother scrubbed the dishes, the girl cleared her throat and asked, "Why do you have some gray hairs?"

The mother paused and looked at her daughter. "Every time you disobey, I get a strand of gray hair."

The mother returned to her task of washing dishes. The little girl stood there, thinking. She cleared her throat again. "Mom?" she said.

"Yes?" her mother answered.

"Why is Grandma's hair all gray?"

Scotty: "Are you a lawyer?"
Attorney: "Yes."
Scotty: "How much do you charge?"
Attorney: "A hundred dollars for four questions."
Scotty: "Isn't that awfully expensive?"
Attorney: "Yes. What's your fourth question?"

⊙⊙⊚

One CEO always scheduled staff meetings for four thirty on Friday afternoons. When one of the employees finally got up the nerve to ask why, the CEO explained, "I'll tell you why—it's the only time of the week when none of you seems to want to argue with me."

⊙⊙⊚

A pizza-shop owner was audited by the IRS.

The agent said, "You have some travel expenses that need to be explained. How do you justify four trips to Rome this year?"

"Oh, I don't need to justify that," replied the shop owner. "Don't you know? We deliver."

Art: "Did you hear the concert on the radio last night?"
Keri: "My radio won't come on at night."
Art: "What's wrong with it?"
Keri: "It's an AM radio."

◉☉◎

Cyberlaw #1: "ASCII stupid question, get a stupid ANSI."
Cyberlaw #2: "All computers wait at precisely the same speed."

◉☉◎

A man at the airline counter tells the woman behind the desk, "I'd like this bag to go to London, this one to Seattle, and this one to Quebec."

"I'm sorry, sir. We can't do that," she replied.

"I'm sure you can," he answered. "That's what you did the last time I flew with you."

"I've had horrible indigestion for the past two days," a patient said.

"And what have you been doing for it?" asked the doctor.

"Taking an antacid twice a day and drinking nothing but milk," said the patient.

"Good—exactly what I would have suggested myself. That'll be fifty dollars."

◉⊙◎

"Have you heard about the amazing new pasta diet?"

"No. What's involved?"

"It's so simple! You simply learn to walk pasta da refrigerator without stopping, and pasta da cookie jar, and pasta da cupboard. . . ."

◉⊙◎

An auto mechanic in the hospital was chatting nervously with his surgeon while being prepped for an operation.

"Sometimes I wish I'd gone into your line of work," he told the doctor. "Everything you doctors do is so cut and dried and tidy. With me, I spend half a day taking an engine apart and putting it back together, and it seems I always have a couple of parts left over."

"Yes," said the surgeon. "I know the feeling."

Why did the ghost join the U.S. Navy?
He wanted to haunt for buried treasure.

⊙⊙⊙

Morgan: "My great-great-great-grandfather fought with General Custer."
Mitchum: "I don't doubt it. Your family'll fight with anybody."

⊙⊙⊙

A rural mail carrier at the end of World War II took the news of the armistice to an isolated mountain family. He thought the good tidings would bring smiles, but the woman on the porch shook her head sadly.

"I s'pose it figures," she grumbled.

"What do you mean?" asked the carrier.

"We sent our Jeb off to join the army two months ago."

"Looks like he missed all the fightin'."

"That's what I mean. That boy never could hold a job."

Teacher: "George, please tell the class what a synonym is."
George: "A synonym means the same thing as the word you
   can't spell."

◉ ⊙ ◎

A third-grade class went to an art museum. The students
were instructed to sit and wait until the guide was ready to
begin the tour. Two boys, however, decided to explore on
their own.

They walked down a hallway and entered a room filled
with modern art pieces.

"Quick, run," said one, "before they say *we* did it!"

◉ ⊙ ◎

It had been snowing for several hours when an announcement
came over the college campus intercom: "Will the students
who are parked on University Drive please move their cars
promptly? We must begin plowing."

Fifteen minutes later, there came another announcement:
"Will the nine hundred students who went to move thirty-
four cars please return to class?"

Knock-knock.
Who's there?
Atch.
Atch who?
Sorry you have a cold.

⊙⊙⊚

Knock-knock.
Who's there?
Dune.
Dune who?
Dune anything in particular this afternoon?

⊙⊙⊚

Knock-knock.
Who's there?
Oswald.
Oswald who?
Oswald-lowed my gum!

One Sunday morning Pastor Bob advised his congregation, "Next week I plan to preach about the sin of lying. In preparation for my message, I want you all to read Mark 17."

The following Sunday the reverend asked for a show of hands from those who had read Mark 17. Every hand went up. Pastor Bob smiled and announced, "Well, Mark has only sixteen chapters. I will now proceed with my sermon on the sin of lying."

◉◉◉

Did you hear the one about the ministers who formed a bowling team? They called themselves the Holy Rollers.

◉◉◉

You Might Be a Preacher If. . .

You've been told to get a real job.
You've been tempted to name your fishing boat *Visitation.*
You couldn't sell used cars.
You never said, "I'm NEVER going to be a preacher!"
You win a door prize at the church banquet, and people say
    it was rigged.
Your belly is ever referred to as "the chicken coop."
Your kids nickname you "Our Father Who Art at a Meeting."

What is a bear's favorite drink?
Koka-Koala.

◉⊙◉

"Are caterpillars good to eat?" asked a little boy at the dinner table.

"No," said his father. "Why would you ask a question like that?"

"Well, there was one in your salad, but it's gone now."

◉⊙◉

A young magician started to work on a cruise ship with his pet parrot. The parrot would always steal his act by saying things like, "The card was up his sleeve!" or "The dove was in his pocket!"

One day the ship sank, and the magician and the parrot found themselves adrift, alone on a lifeboat. For a couple of days, they just sat there looking at each other. Finally, the parrot broke the silence and said, "Okay, I give up. What did you do with the ship?"

Mark Twain once said money is twice tainted: " 'Tain't yours, 'taint mine."

Humorous Headlines:

STUDENTS CRASH INTO TREE RETURNING TO SCHOOL
WOMAN DROWNS IN FOG
MYSTERY SOLVED—DROWNED WOMAN WAS ONLY HIDING

The Reverend Billy Graham tells of a time early in his ministry when he arrived in a small town to preach a revival meeting. Wanting to mail a letter, he asked a young boy where the post office was. When the boy had told him, Dr. Graham thanked him and said, "If you'll come to the church this evening, you can hear me give directions on how to get to heaven."

"I don't think I'll be there," the boy replied. "You don't even know how to get to the post office."

Game Warden: "You're under arrest. You're hunting with last year's license."

Hunter: "But I'm only trying to shoot the deer that got away last year!"

◉⊙◎

Andy came to work limping like crazy. One of his coworkers noticed and asked Andy what happened.

"Oh, nothing," Andy replied. "It's just an old hockey injury that acts up once in a while."

"Gee, I never knew you played hockey," the coworker responded.

"I don't," explained Andy. "I hurt it last year when some stupid official put my favorite player in the penalty box. I put my foot through the television screen."

◉⊙◎

Why did the basketball team flood the gymnasium?
It was the only way they could sink any baskets.

What's the difference between Goldilocks and a genealogist?
A genealogist is interested in forebears.

⊙⊙⊙

Boss: "You drive nails like lightning."
Carpenter: "Pretty fast, huh?"
Boss: "Nope. You never hammer the same place twice."

⊙⊙⊙

Responses to the question, "How is business?"

Tailor: "Oh, it's so-so."
Electrician: "It's fairly light."
Author: "All right."
Farmer: "It's growing."
Astronomer: "Looking up!"
Elevator operator: "Well, it has its ups and downs."
Trash collector: "It's picking up."

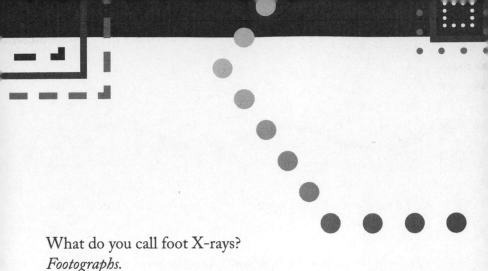

What do you call foot X-rays?
Footographs.

A murderer is condemned to death, but he is allowed to choose how he will be executed. The first choice is to be burned at the stake, the second to be shot by firing squad, and the third to be given over to lions that haven't eaten in two years. Which choice is the best?
The third. Lions that haven't eaten in two years are dead.

Which letter of the alphabet is an island?
T—*you find it in the middle of "water."*

What do you call a cat that sings just like Pavarotti?
Mewsical.

Mozart: "What did the Terminator say to Beethoven?"
Brahms: "Tell me."
Mozart: " 'I'll be Bach!' "

What did the opera singer say to the unexpected guest?
If Aida known you were Carmen, I'd have made something to Nibeling.

When the Smith family moved into their new house, a visiting grandparent asked five-year-old Tommy how he liked the new place.

"It's great," he said. "I have my own room, Alex has his own room, and Jamie has her own room. But poor Mom is still in with Dad."

⊙⊙⊚

Mother: "Why are you crying?"
Mark: "Dad hit his hand with a hammer."
Mother: "I'm surprised you're not laughing."
Mark: "I did."

⊙⊙⊚

A teenaged girl had to stay at her girlfriend's overnight. She was unable to call her parents until the next morning.

"Mom, it's Caroline. I'm fine. My car broke down last night, and by the time I got to Julie's house it was well past midnight. I knew it was too late to call. Please don't be mad at me!"

By now, the woman at the other end of the phone realized the caller had the wrong number. "I'm sorry," she said, "I don't have a daughter named Caroline."

"Oh, Mom! I didn't think you'd be this mad!"

Did you hear about the spider that enrolled in computer courses?

It wanted to learn how to design Web pages.

⊙⊙⊙

A nervous passenger decided to spring for one of those on-the-spot, low-investment-high-benefits insurance policies at the airport before her plane departed. Then she had time for a quick lunch, so she stopped at a Chinese eatery along the terminal walk. Her eyes widened when she read the fortune cookie: "Today's investment will pay big dividends!"

⊙⊙⊙

Mack paid 650 dollars for his gold watch. It was rustproof, shockproof, magnetic proof, fireproof, and, of course, waterproof. There was only one thing wrong with it: He lost it.

Doctor: "After the operation, you'll be a new man."
Patient: "Could you send the bill to the old man?"

◉⊙◎

A man hurried into the emergency room and asked an intern for a cure for the hiccups. The intern grabbed a cup of water and splashed it onto the man's face.

"What in the world did you do that for?" asked the man.

"Well, you don't have the hiccups anymore, do you?" asked the intern.

"No," he replied. "My wife is in the car—she has them."

◉⊙◎

Why do surgeons wear masks during an operation?
So that if any mistake is made, no one will know who did it.

A dying man told his wife he wanted to join the Democratic Party. All his life he'd been a staunch Republican, and his wife wondered why he felt the sudden change in political bent in his final days. His logic: "I want it to be them losing a voter, not us."

President Calvin Coolidge, when pressed by a reporter as to why he was declining to seek reelection, replied, "No chance for advancement."

Have you heard about the new short form for income tax returns? It reads:
1. How much money do you earn?
2. Send it to us.

Day 34

What's the difference between an American student and an English student?
About three thousand miles.

◉⊙◎

The high-school band was nervous. So was the new music teacher. As the band members were preparing for their first concert, the teacher told the kids that if they weren't sure of their part, just to pretend to play.

When the big night arrived, the proud parents waited expectantly. The teacher brought down the baton with a flourish, and lo, the band gave forth with a resounding silence.

◉⊙◎

Student: "I'd like to check out this book on blood clots."
Librarian: "I'm sorry; that doesn't circulate."

Knock-knock.
Who's there?
Howard.
Howard who?
Howard is it to lift a piano?

⊙⊙⊙

Knock-knock.
Who's there?
Butcher.
Butcher who?
Butcher hands up! This is a robbery!

⊙⊙⊙

Knock-knock.
Who's there?
Matthews.
Matthews who?
Matthews are wet. Can I come in and dwy my socks?

Day 36

Reverend Walker was scheduled to perform a special wedding ceremony immediately following the Sunday morning service. He planned to perform the rite before the entire congregation, but for the life of him, he could not remember the names of the two members whom he was to marry. He got around his dilemma this way: "Will those who want to get married now, please come stand before me?"

At once, six single ladies, four widows, and five single men stood, went to the aisle, and walked to the front.

◉◉◉

A Limerick

There was a young girl in the choir
Whose voice went up higher and higher,
Till one Sunday night
It vanished from sight,
And turned up the next day in the spire.

◉◉◉

What excuse did Adam give to his children as to why he no longer lived in Eden?
Your mother ate us out of house and home.

Why did the tiger eat the tightrope walker?
He wanted a well-balanced meal.

◉ ◉ ◉

Mrs. James answered the front doorbell one day to find her dear old friend Mrs. Avery standing outside with a huge, mangy, panting dog. Delighted by the unexpected visit, Mrs. James bade her friend inside. The dog bounded ahead of them, knocked over a valuable vase while dashing for the cat, used the lush carpet as a toilet, then jumped onto an antique sofa and proceeded to take a nap.

He was still napping an hour later when Mrs. Avery rose to leave. Mrs. James showed her to the door and waited for her to call the dog. But her friend paid no attention whatsoever to the animal.

"Aren't you going to take your animal with you?" Mrs. James asked, a hint of impatience in her voice.

"Oh, that awful beast is not my pet. I thought he was yours."

◉ ◉ ◉

What would you get if you crossed a parrot with an elephant?
An animal that tells you everything it remembers.

André Gide once defined art as a collaboration between an artist and God—"And the less the artist does, the better."

⊙⊙⊚

Definitions:

Antique: An item your grandparents bought, your parents got rid of, and you're buying again.
Argument: A fight over who can get in the last word first.
Barium: What we do to most people when they die.
Business Meeting: A time for people to talk about what they're supposed to be doing.
Confidence: The human quality that comes before experience.
Experience: Something you've acquired after it's too late to do you much good.
Sailing: The sport of idling around in circles while you get wet and catch a cold.
Upgrade: A computer program with new and improved bugs.

⊙⊙⊚

"You can observe a lot by just watching." —Yogi Berra

A certain Orlando general manager, discussing his team's 7–27 record: "We can't win at home. We can't win on the road. I just can't figure out where else to play."

The Devils challenged the Angels to a game of cricket.

"But we've got all the players," said the Angels.

"Yes, but we've got all the umpires!" exclaimed the Devils.

A wise old man of the alleys had a profound revelation about the popular sport: "If you can't hear a pin drop, there is something definitely wrong with your bowling."

If you were swimming in the ocean and a big alligator attacked you, what should you do?
Nothing. There are no alligators in the ocean.

⊙⊙⊙

A man rode into town on Monday, stayed five days, and then rode out on Monday. How is this possible?
His horse was named Monday.

⊙⊙⊙

What is the rank of a marine dentist?
Drill Sergeant.

A nonagenarian was interviewed by a local newspaper reporter. "Do you have a lot of great-grandchildren?" the reporter asked.

"To tell the truth," confessed the matriarch, "I expect they're all pretty ordinary."

⦿⊙◎

A mother came inside after gardening and found a big hole in the middle of the pie she had made earlier that morning. She found a gooey spoon lying in the sink and crumbs all over the floor.

She went to find her son. "David," she said, "you promised me that you wouldn't touch the pie I made. And I promised you that if you did touch the pie, I would spank you."

A look of relief came over David. "Now that I've broken my promise," he said, "I think it would be all right for you to break yours, too."

⦿⊙◎

Family friend: "How's your mom? As pretty as ever?"
Kid: "Yeah. It just takes her longer."

What happens when a lightbulb dresses up in a suit of armor?
He becomes a knight light.

◉◉◉

Hickory dickory dock
The mice ran up the clock.
The clock struck one,
And the rest got away with minor injuries.

◉◉◉

What did Cinderella say while she was waiting for her photos?
"Some day my prints will come."

An elderly man took his faithful but weather-beaten Packard to a tune-up shop for an oil change. The two mechanics exchanged glances as the car puttered to a stop at the garage door.

"Man," said one after emitting a low whistle, "I'll bet that thing's still insured against Indian attack."

◉⊙◎

A woman waited at a garage as mechanics scoured her car engine, trying in vain to pinpoint the problem. At length, a parrot in a corner cage sang out, "It's the thermostat."

"We've already checked the thermostat," grumbled one of the mechanics.

"It's the fan belt," the parrot ventured.

"No problem with the fan belt," said the other mechanic.

"It's the heat pump," said the parrot.

"It's not the heat pump!" shouted the first mechanic, exasperated.

The woman was astounded by this exchange. "I've never heard of a bird so intelligent," she said.

"He's completely worthless," countered the second mechanic. "He'll talk your ear off, but he doesn't know the first thing about car engines."

◉⊙◎

Customer: "When I bought this car, you guaranteed that you would fix anything that broke."
Car dealer: "Yes, that's right."
Customer: "Well, I need a new garage."

"I paid more than two thousand dollars to get a cure for my baldness, but I figured it's better to give than to recede."

⊙⊙⊙

An elderly gentleman had serious hearing problems for a number of years. He went to the doctor and was fitted for a set of hearing aids that allowed the man to hear perfectly.

The elderly gentleman went back in a month to the doctor, and the doctor said, "Your hearing is perfect. Your family must be really pleased you can hear again."

The gentleman replied, "Oh, I haven't told my family yet. I just sit around and listen to their conversations. I've changed my will five times!"

⊙⊙⊙

Patient: "Why do you whistle when you operate, Doctor?"
Doctor: "It helps to take my mind off my work."

A secret agent was directed to a posh condominium complex to contact an anonymous source. "Williams is the name," he was told by his superior. "Hand him this envelope."

Arriving at the complex, he was confused to find four different Williamses occupying adjacent quarters. He decided to try the second condo. When a gentleman answered his knock, the agent spoke the pass code: "The grape arbor is down."

Looking him over, the man shook his head. "I'm Williams the accountant. You might try Williams the spy. Two doors down."

⊙⊙⊙

Did you hear about the lamb that called the police? He had been fleeced.

⊙⊙⊙

An Amish man in Lancaster County was arrested because the red lantern on the back of his buggy blew out. When he was taken to jail, he was told he could make one phone call. But who was he to call? None of his friends or family had telephones.

Voted "Most Likely to Succeed":

Porcupines—they're sharp.
Fireflies—they're bright.
Rabbits—they're great at multiplying.
Hummingbirds—they finish their hum-work.
Cats—they get purr-fect grades.
Elephants—they have lots of gray matter.

⊙⊙⊙

The students in the chemistry class were watching the professor give a demonstration of the properties of various acids. "Now," said the professor, "I am going to drop a silver dollar into this glass of acid. Will it dissolve?"

"No, sir," answered one of the students.

"No?" quizzed the professor. "Could you explain to the class why it won't dissolve?"

"Because," the student replied, "if the money would dissolve, then you wouldn't drop it in."

⊙⊙⊙

Definitions:

Graduate School: The approximate point at which a university student ceases dependency on parents and commences dependency on spouse.

Money: A device by which parents stay in touch with their college children.

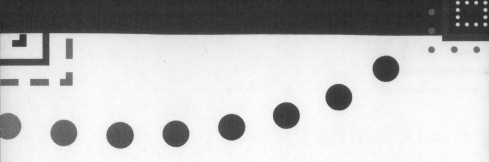

Knock-knock.
Who's there?
Midas.
Midas who?
Midas well let me in. I'm not going anywhere.

⊙⊙⊙

Knock-knock.
Who's there?
Sam and Janet.
Sam and Janet who?
Sam and Janet evening.

⊙⊙⊙

Knock-knock.
Who's there?
Noah.
Noah who?
Noah good air freshener that'll work on a boat?

First Baptist has instigated a summer special day—Old Timers' Sunday. This year farmer John Calver brought in his horse and carriage with a hand-lettered sign: ENERGY-EFFICIENT VEHICLE. RUNS ON OATS AND GRASS. CAUTION: DO NOT STEP IN EXHAUST.

⊙⊙⊙

Pastor father: "I never kissed a girl before I married your mother. Will you be able to tell your children that?"
Parsonage son: "Not with a straight face."

⊙⊙⊙

A rather stingy man died and went to heaven. He was met at the front gate by St. Peter, who led him on a house tour down the golden streets. They passed mansion after beautiful mansion until they came to the end of the street and stopped in front of a tiny shack without gold paving in front.

"And here is where you will be living, sir," Peter announced.

"Me, live here?" the stingy man yelled. "How come?"

Peter replied, "I did the best I could with the money you sent us."

What does the lion say to his friends before they go out hunting for food?
"Let us prey."

⊙⊙⊙

A panda bear walked into a restaurant and ordered a sandwich. When he received the sandwich, he ate it and then took out a gun, shot a hole in the ceiling, and left the restaurant.

A policeman caught up with the panda and told him he had broken the law. The panda bear told the policeman that he was innocent, and, if he didn't believe him, to look in the dictionary. The policeman got a dictionary and looked up *panda bear*.

The entry read, "Panda Bear: Eats shoots and leaves."

⊙⊙⊙

What do you call a dinosaur that steps on everything in its way?
Tyrannosaurus wrecks.

Which composer is squirrels' all-time favorite?
Tchaikovsky. He wrote "The Nutcracker."

⊙⊙⊙

"Can you carry a tune at all?" the grumpy talent agent asked the final person trying out after a long day of auditions.

"I'll let you judge that for yourself." The person auditioning confidently launched into a terrible, loud rendition of a well-known popular song.

"Well, what do you think? Can I carry a tune?"

"Yes," said the agent. "Please carry it out and close the door behind you."

⊙⊙⊙

Bert: "Why do you keep singing the same song over and over?"
Gert: "The melody haunts me."
Bert: "That's because you're murdering it!"

Bill: "Which do you think is America's worst problem: ignorance or apathy?"

Lil: "Don't know. Don't really care, either."

◉◉◎

Shaquille O'Neal, on his lack of championships: "I've won at every level except college and pro."

O'Neal on whether he had visited the Parthenon during his visit to Greece: "I can't really remember the names of the clubs that we went to."

◉◉◎

News never is really news. It just happens to different people from day to day.

Baseball One-Liners:

I was watching a baseball game on television when my wife said, "Speaking of high and outside, the grass needs to be mowed."

That free agent doesn't steal bases, he buys them.

I like the good old days when umpires called strikes and the player's union didn't.

The only problem he has in the outfield is with fly balls.

Baseball will outlast all other sports because a diamond is forever.

⊙⊙⊙

Les: "Why don't rugby players have midlife crises?"
Tess: "They stay stuck in adolescence."

⊙⊙⊙

The crowd was mercilessly jeering and heckling the referee in a high-school match. Finally, the poor official walked over to the bleachers and sat down next to his loudest critic.

"What are you doing?" asked the spectator.

"Well," said the ref, "it seems you get the best view from here."

Why did the archaeologist go bankrupt?
Because his career was in ruins.

◉⊙◉

The shopkeeper was discouraged when a new business much like his own opened up next door and erected a huge sign that read, BEST DEALS.

He was depressed when another competitor opened up on the block and announced its arrival with an even larger sign reading, LOWEST PRICES.

The shopkeeper was panicked until he got an idea. He put the biggest sign of all over his own shop—it read, MAIN ENTRANCE.

◉⊙◉

Ed: "I have a job in a watch factory."
Mike: "Oh really? What do you do?"
Ed: "I just stand around and make faces."

Why can't a woman ask for help from her brother?
He can't be a brother and assist her, too.

◉◉◉

Once upon a time, there was a clever thief charged with treason against the king and sentenced to die. However, the king decided to be a little merciful and let the thief choose which way he would die. Which way should he choose?
He should choose to die of old age.

◉◉◉

What is the difference between a kangaroo and a mailbox?
If you don't know, I am not sending you to mail these letters!

Once there was a millionaire who had a collection of alligators. He kept them in the pool behind his mansion. The millionaire also had a very beautiful daughter who was single. One day he decided to throw a huge party, and during the course of the party he announced, "Ladies and Gentlemen, I have a proposition for every man here. I will give one million dollars or my daughter to the man who can swim across this pool full of alligators and emerge alive!"

As soon as he finished, there was a large *splash*. There was one man in the pool, swimming with all his might and screaming in fear. The crowd cheered him on as he sprinted through the water. Finally, he jumped out on the other side with only a torn shirt and minor injuries. The millionaire was awestruck.

He said, "Sir, that was amazing! I didn't think it could be done! But I must keep my end of the bargain. Do you want my daughter or the one million dollars?"

The guy answered, "I don't want your money or your daughter. I just want the person who pushed me into the water!"

◉⊙◎

A father was showing pictures of his wedding day to his son. "Is that when Mommy came to work for us?" the boy asked.

◉⊙◎

Fern: "Oh, I wish I'd listened to my mother."
Ivy: "Why? What did she tell you?"
Fern: "I don't know, I wasn't listening."

A tourist was driving down a desert road and came upon a sign that read, ROAD CLOSED. DO NOT ENTER. He thought the road looked passable, so he ignored the sign and continued driving down the road.

A mile later, he came to a bridge that was out. He turned around and drove back in the direction he came from. As he approached the warning sign, he read on the other side: WELCOME BACK. TOLD YOU SO!

◉◉◉

A man went to the airline counter. The ticket agent asked, "Sir, do you have reservations?"

He replied, "Reservations? Of course I have reservations, but I'm flying anyway."

◉◉◉

"What kinds of papers do I need to travel to Europe?" a youth asked a travel agent.

"Basically, a passport and a visa."

"I have the passport, no problem. Do you think they'll accept Mastercard?"

Bill Vaughn, in the *Kansas City Star*: "Know what? The trouble with the average family is it has too much month left over at the end of the money."

◉◉◉

Farmer Adams was bragging to farmer Black. "I really had a fine day at the market. Guess how many watermelons I sold?"

" 'Bout half, I s'pose."

"Half? Half what?"

"Half as many as you're about to claim."

◉◉◉

Sign in a department store window in May: ONLY 224 SHOPPING DAYS LEFT UNTIL CHRISTMAS!

Dad: "I think Junior's planning to become an astronaut."
Mom: "What makes you think so?"
Dad: "He spends every day sitting in a chair, staring into space."

⊙⊙⊙

Where do space explorers leave their spacecraft?
At parking meteors.

⊙⊙⊙

A man wrote to his local meteorologist: "I thought you may be interested in knowing that I shoveled eighteen inches of 'partly cloudy' from my sidewalk this morning."

Where was the Declaration of Independence signed?
On the bottom.

⊙⊙⊚

Teacher: "What happened in 1809?"
Eddie: "Abraham Lincoln was born."
Teacher: "Right. Now, what happened in 1812?"
Eddie: "He turned three years old."

⊙⊙⊚

"Who invented the bow and arrow?" asked the teacher.
"Cavemen!" cried Gary enthusiastically.
"Cavemen? And what do you suppose prompted cavemen to come up with the bow and arrow?"
"Er. . .somebody kept stealing the wheel?"

Voted "Most Likely to Fail":

Squids—they can't ink straight.
Gorillas—they monkey around too much.
Mice—they just squeak by.
Cows—they copy off each udder.
Turtles—they're always late to class.
Lizards—they are always losing their newt-books.
Squirrels—they drive the teacher nuts.
Parrots—they keep repeating their first year.

◉⊙◎

Did you hear about the delivery van loaded with thesauruses that crashed into a bus? Witnesses were shocked, astounded, surprised, taken aback, dumbfounded, thunderstruck, startled, caught unaware....

◉⊙◎

College student: "Hey, Dad! I've got some great news for you!"
Father: "What, son?"
College student: "Remember that five hundred dollars you promised me if I made the Dean's list?"
Father: "I certainly do."
College student: "Well, you get to keep it."

Knock-knock.
Who's there?
Anita.
Anita who?
Anita flashlight so I can see in the dark!

⊙⊙⊙

Knock-knock.
Who's there?
Figs.
Figs who?
Figs the doorbell; it's broken.

⊙⊙⊙

Knock-knock.
Who's there?
Sam the drummer.
Beat it.

Day 62

Judge: "Don't you want a lawyer to represent you?"
Defendant: "Naw, I've decided to tell the truth."

◉◉◉

A couple gaped at the television as they watched their lawyer being interviewed during a newscast. The reporter wanted the attorney's comments for a local angle in a late-breaking Supreme Court decision.

"I wonder how in the world she got hold of our lawyer," the husband said, shaking his head. "I've been trying to get him to update our will for the last three weeks, and his secretary invariably says he's with clients."

◉◉◉

A lawyer was reading the will of a wealthy, deceased client to the assembled beneficiaries. "And I always promised to mention my lazy nephew Larry in my will. Hi there, Larry. . . ."

Hoping to help his church save money, Pastor Jones decided to paint the church exterior himself, but all he had on hand was one bucket of paint. So he collected a bunch of empty buckets and some water, which he used to thin the paint enough to cover the building. Then he spent the whole day painting.

That night it rained and washed off all the paint. The pastor was so discouraged and asked God, "Why. . .why, Lord, did you let it rain and wash away all my hard work?"

To which God replied, "Repaint and thin no more!"

◎◉◎

Pete: "Who was the greatest financier in the Bible?"
Zach: "Noah. He was floating his stock while everyone else was in liquidation."

◎◉◎

Sunday school teacher: "Do you remember your memory verse, Charlie?"
Charlie: "I sure do. I even remember the zip code. . .John 3:16."

What does a thirty-pound rat say?
"Here, kitty-kitty. . . ."

Camel 1: "How is life treating you?"
Camel 2: "I've had hard times, but I'm finally getting over the hump."

Why are dolphins more clever than humans?
Within three hours they can train a person to stand beside a pool and feed them fish.

Tell a man there are three hundred billion stars in the universe, and he believes you. Tell him a bench has wet paint on it, and he has to touch it to be sure.

◉◉◉

Humorous Headlines:

Suspect Says He Fired Gun to Frighten Deceased
Elderly Man Slips in Bathtub, Breaks New Year's
    Resolution
Car Hits Jaywalker with No Headlights
Woman Expected to Recover from Fatal Crash

◉◉◉

It was the late Senator Everett Dirksen who quipped, "A billion here, a billion there. . . Pretty soon, you're talking about real money."

Day
66

Knock-knock.
Who's there?
Tijuana.
Tijuana who?
Tijuana shoot some hoops later?

◉◉◉

Written on a boxer's tombstone: You Can Stop Counting. I'm Not Getting Up.

◉◉◉

These days many people get their exercise by jumping to conclusions, flying off the handle, dodging responsibility, bending the rules, running down everything, circulating rumors, passing the buck, stirring up trouble, shooting the bull, digging up dirt, slinging mud, throwing their weight around, beating the system, pushing their luck, kicking the system, and stooping to less-than-godly behavior.

Day 67

The more you take away, the bigger it gets—what is it?
A hole.

⊙⊙⊙

If George Washington went to Washington wearing a white winter coat while his wife waited in Wilmington, how many *W*s are there in all?
None. There are no Ws *in the word* all.

⊙⊙⊙

What do you get when you mix poison ivy with a four-leaf clover?
A rash of good luck.

Ms. Crocker: "This cookbook shows you how to serve your family balanced meals."

Jenny: "Oh. I'm already doing that. One day my husband complains, and the next day the kids complain."

Ms. Crocker: "Another thing, my dear, when you serve the guests at dinner, be careful not to spill anything."

Jenny: "Not me! I won't say a word!"

◉⊙◎

A three-year-old went with his dad to see a litter of kittens. On returning home, he breathlessly told his mom there were two boy kittens and two girl kittens.

"How did you know which were which?" his mom asked.

"Daddy picked them up and looked underneath," the boy replied. "I think it's printed on the bottom."

◉⊙◎

Bob: "I got a practically new BMW for my wife."

Bill: "Wow! I'd like to make a trade like that."

Ted: "What's this?"
Jane: "It's dessert. I made it."
Ted: "What do you call it?"
Jane: "That's pound cake, silly!"
Ted: "Oh. I can see why."
Jane: "What do you mean?"
Ted: "I'll need a hammer to pound out the lumps."

◉◉◉

What kind of food will you find in heaven?
Angel food cake.

◉◉◉

"I thought you were going to count calories," Lois gently reminded her friend Karla as she consumed her second milkshake.

"Oh, I am," said Karla. "So far today, I'm at 5,760."

Two information-services managers were complaining about their work:

"If our computers could think for themselves, my problems would be over," said one.

"If my technical staff could think for itself, so would mine," said the other.

⊙⊙⊙

Why did the lamb like its computer?
It was ewe-ser friendly.

⊙⊙⊙

The clerk had had it up to the hair follicles with the office computer, which seemed to crash every ten minutes. Hours of futile phone calls to tech support and long waits on permahold yielded no solutions. Finally, she managed to contact one of the programmers of the software she was using. She gave the programmer a detailed description of the problems, concluding, "And that manual of yours is no help at all. We can't understand a word it says."

The programmer was less than remorseful. "That's all to be expected."

"To be expected!? We paid good money for this!"

"Of course. It's a good program. It was a very difficult program to write. Why do you think it should be easy to understand?"

Patient: "Doctor, I don't know what's wrong with me—I hurt all over. If I touch my shoulder here, I hurt, and if I touch my leg here, I hurt, and if I touch my head here, I hurt, and if I touch my foot here, I hurt."

Doctor: "I believe your finger is broken."

⊙⊙⊙

Why wouldn't the duck go to the duck doctor?
Because he was a quack.

⊙⊙⊙

Definitions:

Acupuncturist: A Chinese doctor who quietly does his jab.
Hospital: The place to wind up people who are run down.
Orthodontist: A doctor who braces children and straps parents.

During a training exercise, an army unit was late for afternoon inspection.

"Where are those camouflage trucks?" the irate colonel barked.

"They're around here somewhere. . . ," replied the sergeant.

◉⊙◎

What fruit is often hired by the navy?
Naval oranges.

◉⊙◎

Mrs. Green: "My daughter's marrying a military man—a second lieutenant."
Mrs. Gray: "So, she let the first one get away?"

What's the difference between a cat and a comma?
One has the paws before the claws, and the other has the clause before the pause.

◉ ◉ ◉

Definition:

Phonetic: An example of a word that isn't spelled the way it sounds.

◉ ◉ ◉

Tips to Improve Your Writing:
- Avoid alliteration. Always.
- Never use a long word when a diminutive one will do.
- Employ the vernacular.
- Avoid ampersands & abbreviations, etc.
- Parenthetical remarks (however relevant) are unnecessary.
- Remember to never split an infinitive.
- Foreign words and phrases are not *apropos.*
- One should never generalize.
- Don't be redundant; don't use more words than necessary; it's highly superfluous.
- Analogies in writing are like feathers on a snake.
- Poofread carefully to see if you words or letters out.
- A writer must not shift your point of view.
- Place pronouns as close as possible, especially in long sentences, as of ten or more words, to the antecedents.
- Writing carefully, dangling participles must be avoided.
- Every person should be careful to use a singular pronoun with singular nouns in their writing.

Knock-knock.
Who's there?
Pecan.
Pecan who?
Pecan someone your own size.

⊙⊙⊚

Knock-knock!
Who's there?
Osborn.
Osborn who?
Osborn way up in the heels.

⊙⊙⊚

Knock-knock.
Who's there?
Juneau.
Juneau who?
Juneau I was your next-door neighbor?

"The difference between dating and marrying," a father advised his college son, "is a matter of expectations."

"What do you mean, Dad?"

"You take your girl out to dinner, for example. She appreciates it. You take your wife out to dinner—she expects it."

⊙⊙⊙

Henry knelt in front of his girl Henrietta and pleaded, "I've told you before and I'll tell you again: I just can't live without you."

"Yeah, I heard you the first time, and all the other times," she replied. "I would think you'd be dead by now."

⊙⊙⊙

Young Miss Jones: "I'm going out with Joe tonight."

Mama Jones: "Joe again? If you like his attention so much, why don't you marry him?"

Young Miss Jones: "Because I like his attention."

How are a lawyer and an escaped prisoner similar?
They both had to pass the bars.

◉☉◉

Man: "You really should let Frank represent you in this lawsuit."

Lady: "Frank! Why, he graduated at the bottom of his law-school class. I don't think he ever won a case."

Man: "True, but he'll lose for you cheaper than anyone else in town."

◉☉◉

Why did the cucumber need a lawyer?
It was in a pickle.

The story is told of Daniel Webster who, after a day of hunting, found himself far from home at nightfall. After groping through the darkness awhile, he came upon a farmhouse and knocked repeatedly at the door. It was several minutes before the farmer opened an upstairs window and held a lantern out to see who was down there.

"What do you want?" the farmer asked gruffly.

"I wish to spend the night here," Webster implored.

"Good. Spend the night there." The lantern went out and the window closed.

◉⊙◎

Who was the basketball player's favorite poet?
Longfellow.

◉⊙◎

Spike: "My bro's a boxer."
Ike: "Oh yeah? What's his fightin' name?"
Spike: "Van Gogh, because he's always on the canvas."

How many federal employees does it take to screw in a lightbulb?
None. Lightbulbs have been cut from the budget.

⊙⊙⊙

A woman had been waiting in line more than an hour at the tax office. "If they didn't give us so much red tape to go through," she fumed to no one in particular, "both the government and the taxpayers would be better off."

A bedraggled clerk overheard the remark and snapped, "If we want your opinion, we will provide you with the appropriate form to complete."

⊙⊙⊙

Why was Snow White elected to the Supreme Court?
She was the fairest of them all.

Sister Smith invited the children to come to the front for the children's sermon. She had prepared an object lesson using squirrels as an example of industry and planning ahead. She requested that the boys and girls raise their hands when they knew what she was describing.

"This thing lives in trees [pause] and eats nuts [pause]." No hands went up. "It is gray [pause] and has a long bushy tail [pause]." The children looked at each other, but no hands were raised. "And it jumps from branch to branch [pause] and chatters when it gets excited [pause]."

Finally a little boy tentatively raised his hand. Sister Smith breathed a sigh of relief and called on him. "Well," he said, "I know the answer must be Jesus, but it sure sounds more like a squirrel to me."

◉ ◉ ◉

Who was the most popular Old Testament actor?
Samson, who brought down the house.

◉ ◉ ◉

"Most people are bothered by those passages of scripture they do not understand, but the passages that bother me are those I do understand." —Mark Twain

"Oh, no! The weather forecaster is calling for rain!" the kangaroo groaned to the rabbit.

"What's the problem with that?" asked the rabbit. "We could use some rain."

"Yes, but that means my children will have to stay inside to play."

◉ ◉ ◉

What do you call a grizzly bear with no teeth?
A gummy bear.

◉ ◉ ◉

There was once a lazy alligator that roamed the banks of the river. Whenever a boat passed him, those onboard would be sure to keep their hands inside the vessel, because it was known that he was always looking for a handout.

"Everyone thinks their family was rather boring, but mine really was. We had a coffee table book titled *Pictures We Took Just to Use Up the Rest of the Film*." —Fred Allen

◉ ⊙ ◎

What do you get if you cross Glenn Miller with dynamite?
A blast from the past.

◉ ⊙ ◎

Jay Leno observing the food habits of Americans: "Do you remember when they said movie popcorn is bad for you, and the same for Chinese food? They now say that sandwiches are bad for you because of the high fat content. Anything with mayo, cheese, or meat is bad for you. Do you realize that all those years when you were a kid and you carried your lunch to school, the Twinkie was probably the healthiest thing in there?"

Sam: "How many NCAA basketball players does it take to change a lightbulb?"

Mike: "Only one. But he gets money, a car, and three credit hours for doing it."

◉◉◉

"I don't believe for a second that weight lifting is a sport. They pick up a heavy thing and put it down again. I call that indecision."

◉◉◉

The Politically Correct National Football League announces its name changes and schedules for the season:

The Washington Native Americans will host the New York Very Tall People on opening day.

Other key games include the Dallas Western-Style Laborers versus the St. Louis Uninvited Guests, and the Minnesota Plundering Norsemen versus the Green Bay Meat Industry Workers.

In week two, there are several key matchups, highlighted by the showdown between the San Francisco Precious Metal Enthusiasts and the New Orleans Good People. Also, the Atlanta Birds of Prey versus the Philadelphia National Birds of Symbolic Patriotism, and the Seattle Birds of Prey versus the Phoenix Male Finches.

The Monday night game will pit the Miami Pelagic Percoid Food Fishes against the Denver Untamed Beasts of Burden, the Cincinnati Large Bangladeshi Carnivorous Mammals versus Tampa Bay's West Indies Free Booters, and the Detroit Large Carnivorous Cats versus the Chicago Security-Traders-in-a-Declining-Market.

Week nine will feature the Indianapolis Young Male Horses versus New England Zealous Lovers of Country.

What goes up and down but doesn't move?
A staircase.

⊙⊙⊙

A man was found murdered on Sunday morning. His wife immediately notified the police. The police questioned the wife and staff and compiled these alibis:

The wife said she was sleeping.
The cook was cooking breakfast.
The maid was gathering vegetables.
The butler was getting the mail.

The police instantly arrested the murderer. Who did it and how did they know?
It was the butler. He said he was getting the mail, but there is no mail on Sunday!

⊙⊙⊙

What do you get when you cross a robber and a shark?
A bite out of crime.

Frank: "Well, Ted, you've certainly come up in the world. You're playing golf with two caddies."
Ted: "Oh, it was my wife's idea."
Frank: "Your wife?"
Ted: "Yeah. She thought I ought to spend more time with the kids."

◉⊙◎

Forecast for mothers-to-be: Showers expected.

◉⊙◎

Things You'll Never Hear Your Redneck Cousin Say:

"Duct tape won't fix that."
"I thought Graceland was tacky."
"No kids in the back of the pickup; it's not safe."
"I just couldn't find a thing at Wal-Mart today."
"Little Debbie snack cakes have too many saturated fats."
"Elvis who?"
"Hey, here's an episode of *Hee-Haw* that we haven't seen."
"The tires on that truck are too big."
"We're vegetarians."

Two street people were being entertained watching a teenager try to park a car across the street. The space was ample, but the driver just couldn't maneuver the car into it. Traffic was jammed. Angry drivers honked, further flabbergasting the poor youth. It took a full five minutes before the car was in place.

"That," said one of the idlers, "is what you call paralyzed parking."

◉◉◉

If Santa rode a motorcycle, what kind would it be?
A Holly Davidson.

◉◉◉

A lady aboard a cruise ship was not impressed by the jazz trio in one of the shipboard restaurants. When her waiter came around, she asked, "Will they play anything I ask?"

"Of course, Madam."

"Then tell them to go play shuffleboard."

If an apple a day keeps the doctor away, what will an onion do?
Keep everyone away.

⊙⊙⊙

Lisa: "I've heard that a milk bath is good for the skin, so I'll
    need enough to fill the tub."
Grocer: "Pasteurized?"
Lisa: "No, just up to my chin will do."

⊙⊙⊙

What is the best exercise for losing weight?
Pushing yourself away from the table.

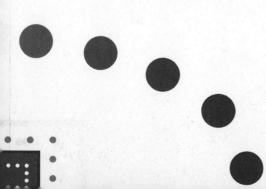

Day 87

An overzealous traffic cop stopped a country vicar making his rounds on his bicycle. After checking the bike thoroughly and finding nothing, he had to let the cleric go.

"You will never arrest me," declared the vicar, "because God is with me wherever I go."

"Well, then," said the cop, "I'm ticketing you for carrying a passenger on a single-seat vehicle."

◉◉◉

What do polite prisoners say when they bump into someone?
"Pardon me."

◉◉◉

Chris: "Uh-oh. I just made an illegal left turn."
Mike: "That's okay. The police car behind you did the same thing."

Did you ever wonder how, according to advertised statistics, two out of three American doctors can recommend one pain reliever while three out of four doctors recommend a rival, and four out of five doctors simultaneously recommend yet a third brand?

◉⊙◎

Definitions:

Bank: A place where you can borrow money—provided you can prove you don't need to.

Best Man: The one the bride doesn't marry.

Diplomacy: The art of saying "Nice dog!" until you can get your hands on a stick.

Dodgers: Jaywalkers in Los Angeles.

Gossiper: Someone with a lively sense of rumor.

Horse Sense: Stable thinking.

Perfectionist: A person who goes to infinite pains and spreads them to the people nearby.

Shin: The human bone most useful for finding hard obstacles in the dark.

◉⊙◎

A running back in New Orleans, anticipating the new season, is quoted as saying, "I want to rush for one thousand or fifteen hundred yards, whichever comes first."

Manuel: "Do you think anyone can really tell the future with cards?"

Todd: "My mom can. She took a look at my report card and told me exactly what was going to happen when my dad got home."

⊙⊙⊙

Teacher: "Shirley, compose a sentence that begins with 'I.'"

Shirley: "I is—"

Teacher: "Never say, 'I is.' It's 'He is' or 'She is,' but 'I am.' Begin your sentence, 'I am. . .'"

Shirley: "I am the ninth letter of the alphabet."

⊙⊙⊙

"I have good news and bad news," said the teacher. "The good news is that we're having only half a day of school this morning."

The class went wild with joy until the teacher quieted them.

"The bad news," he said, "is that we'll have the other half this afternoon."

Knock-knock
Who's there?
Amanda.
Amanda who?
Amanda fix your television set.

Knock-knock.
Who's there?
Ida.
Ida who?
Ida called you first, but my phone is dead.

Knock-knock.
Who's there?
Candace.
Candace who?
Candace be the last knock-knock joke?
(NO!)

In an elevator:

Passenger: "I guess your job has its ups and downs, heh, heh."

Elevator operator: "I don't mind the ups and downs. It's the jerks I can't stand!"

◉◉◉

Show me a coal miner who wears a flashlight on his helmet, and I'll show you a guy whose work makes him lightheaded.

◉◉◉

Why was the employee fired from the orange juice factory? *He couldn't concentrate.*

A Sunday school teacher asked her little students, as they were on the way to the church service, "And why should we be quiet in church?"

A little girl replied, "Because people are sleeping."

◉⊙◎

How many missionaries does it take to change a lightbulb? *One, and thirty natives to see the light.*

◉⊙◎

Adam: "Do you really love me?"
Eve: "There's no one but you."

How does a dog turn off the VCR?
He presses the PAWS button.

⊙⊙⊙

A mother, much against her better judgment, finally gave in and bought the children a dog with the understanding that they would care for it. They named the dog Laddy. It wasn't long before the responsibility fell to the mother, and she found that she was taking care of the dog all by herself. Since the children did not live up to their promise, she decided to sell Laddy.

One of them sorrowfully said, "We'll miss him."

Another said, "If he wouldn't eat so much and wouldn't be so messy, could we please keep him?"

Mom stood strong and held her ground. "It's time to take Laddy to his new home."

"*Laddy?*" the children asked. "We thought you said *Daddy.*"

⊙⊙⊙

What kind of trees do puppies like best?
Dogwood. They like its bark.

Day
94

What did the Old Woman Who Lived in a Shoe require more than anything else?
A babysitter.

Knock-knock.
Who's there?
Aesop.
Aesop who?
Aesop I saw a puddy tat.

What happens when a king burps?
He issues a royal pardon.

Day 95

Brett: "Do you have holes in your socks?"
Jim: "Certainly not!"
Brett: "Then how do you get your feet in them?"

◉⊙◎

A man was watching a football game when his wife returned from the mall, loaded down with bags.

"I thought you were only going window-shopping," he said.

"Yes, I bought the curtains for the kitchen window, but I got a few things that match them: a can opener, a coffee maker, a blender. . . ."

◉⊙◎

Getting away from their high-stress jobs, May and Trey spend relaxing weekends in their motor home. When they found their peace and quiet disturbed by well-meaning but unwelcome visits from other campers, they devised a plan to assure their privacy.

Now when they set up camp, they place this sign on their RV door: INSURANCE AGENT. ASK ABOUT OUR TERM-LIFE PACKAGE.

Guide: "I never guide hunters anymore, just fishermen."
Hunter: "Why?"
Guide: "I've never been mistaken for fish."

Terry and Gus are at the office watercooler, talking about horse racing. Terry is going on and on about how he understands the sport and always wins at the track. When he finally gets around to asking Gus what happens to the horses he follows, Gus says, "The horses I follow usually end up following the other horses."

Tennis Quips:

To err is human. To put the blame on someone else is doubles.
Never marry a tennis player, because to him love means nothing.

Ancient Roman magicians used an ingenious method for walking through solid walls. What was it?
A door.

⊙⊙⊙

A man is locked in a room with no way to get out. In the room there is a piano, a baseball bat, a saw, and a table. How could he get out?
He could take a key from the piano and unlock the door.
He could take the bat and get three strikes. Then he'd be out.
He could take the saw and cut the table in two. Then, by putting the two halves together, he would have a "hole" and he could get out.

⊙⊙⊙

What can you hold without touching it?
Your breath.

Day
98

Big sister: "Mom says babies are expensive."
Big brother: "Yes, but think how long they last."

◉◉◉

A little boy returned from grocery shopping with his mom. While his mother put away the groceries, the little boy opened his box of animal crackers and spread them out all over the kitchen table.

"What are you doing?" asked his mom.

"The box says you shouldn't eat them if the seal is broken," said the little boy. "I'm looking for the seal."

◉◉◉

"What's the most difficult age to get a child to sleep regularly?" a new mother asked an older veteran of child rearing.

"About seventeen years."

"I've never flown before," a nervous old lady told the pilot. "You will bring me down safely, won't you?"

"All I can say, ma'am," said the pilot, "is that I've never left anyone up there yet!"

⊙⊙⊙

A stout businessman took his suitcase from the luggage ramp at the Fresno airport and huffed to the airline's courtesy desk. "What's the meaning of this?" he demanded, showing the agent the large, red-lettered handling tag tied to his suitcase handle. "I'm well aware of my weight problem, but what right does your airline have to comment on it in public?"

The agent read the tag: *FAT*.

"That," she explained, "is the destination code for this airport."

⊙⊙⊙

"I just returned from Germany and had the most wonderful time," bubbled Ginger to her friends.

"I thought before you left, you said you were having trouble with your German," Melody said.

"Oh, I spoke fluently. It was the Germans who had trouble with it."

Why did Lois Lane meet Superman at the ice cream shop?
She was hoping for a scoop.

Knock-knock.
Who's there?
Quiche.
Quiche who?
Dracula gives the quiche of death!

Why did Snoopy quit his job?
He was tired of working for Peanuts!

A woman was sharing with a friend her husband's state of mind: "Walter's psychiatrist has done him a world of good. He used to refuse to answer the phone when it rang. Now he answers it even when it doesn't ring."

◉◉◉

Definition:

Dentist's Office: A filling station.

◉◉◉

Doctor: "I want you to drink plenty of liquids so you'll get over this cold."
Mrs. Martin: "I never drink anything else."

The new army recruits were rousted out of their bunks at 3:30 a.m. "You're wasting the best part of the day already!" screamed the sergeant.

One recruit turned to another and muttered, "It sure doesn't take long to spend the night around here."

◉⊙◎

When Philip of Macedon was conquering Greece, he encountered only one stronghold of real resistance: the city of Sparta. Hoping to convince the Spartans to surrender without the loss of more soldiers, he sent a messenger warning of all the ravages that would come if Philip's army had to take the city by force.

Sparta's reply was one word in length: "If."

Impressed by their confidence, Philip left the city alone.

◉⊙◎

"We received our uniforms today," a recruit wrote to his mother from boot camp. "It made me feel very proud, although the pants are a little too loose around the chest."

"I think Thomas Edison must have been the most brilliant person who ever lived," said Kate.

"What makes you think so?" asked her teacher.

"He invented the lightbulb. Then, to give people a reason to keep the lights on all night, he invented the phonograph!"

⊙⊙⊙

Which vegetable wasn't allowed on Columbus's ships?
The leek.

⊙⊙⊙

History Teacher: "Why was George Washington standing in the bow of the boat as the army crossed the Delaware?"
Student: "Because he knew if he sat down, he would have to row."

Father: "I pay your tuition at the Sorbonne, and when I ask you to show me what you've learned, you take me to a fancy restaurant and speak to the waiter in French. You call this a valuable education?"

Sam: "Sure, Dad. I told him to give you the check."

⊙ ⊙ ⊙

An eighth-grade student was having difficulty completing his homework. Finally he slammed his textbook shut, threw down his pencil, and informed his parents, "I've decided I'm a conscientious objector."

"Why did you decide that?" asked his mother.

"Because wars create too much history!"

⊙ ⊙ ⊙

Father: "How are your grades, Peter?"

Peter: "They're underwater, Dad."

Father: "What do you mean, underwater?"

Peter: "They're below C level."

Knock-knock.
Who's there?
Desdemona.
Desdemona who?
Desdemona Lisa still hang in Paris?

○⊙◎

Knock-knock.
Who's there?
Nobel.
Nobel who?
Nobel, so I knocked.

○⊙◎

Knock-knock.
Who's there?
Midas.
Midas who?
Midas well sit down.

Day 106

How do preachers communicate with each other?
Parson to parson.

⊙⊙⊙

A Sunday school teacher was reading a Bible story to her class. "The man named Lot was warned to take his wife and flee out of the city, but his wife looked back and turned to salt."

A little boy softly asked, "What happened to the flea?"

⊙⊙⊙

A new employee was being shown the ropes at the office.

"What our management looks for more than anything else," said the supervisor, "is for everyone here to be methodical. You can get by with a few deficiencies in other regards, but you absolutely *must* be methodical."

The newcomer, stunned, said, "Well, I may as well turn in my resignation right now."

"But you haven't even started work!"

"No, and I don't plan to. I've been a deepwater Baptist all my life, and I don't see any good reason to become a Methodical at this point in time."

What vegetable do you get when an elephant walks through your garden?
Squash.

⊙⊙⊚

A pet-shop owner was trying to talk Mrs. McClellan into buying a bulldog for her children. "Oh, they'll love this little rascal!" said the clerk. "He's full of fun and he eats anything. He especially likes children."

⊙⊙⊚

Three animals were having a disagreement over who was the best: The first, a hawk, claimed that because of his ability to fly, he was able to attack anything repeatedly from above, and his prey didn't have a chance.

The second, a lion, based his claim on his strength—none in the forest dared to challenge him.

The third, a skunk, insisted he did not need either flight or strength to ward off any creature.

As the trio argued, a grizzly bear came along and swallowed them all: hawk, lion, and stinker!

The politician concluded a boisterous but shallow speech filled with impossible promises sure to appeal to the particular audience. Mingling with the crowd, he happened on a wise, respected old city father. Hoping for a compliment within hearing of some of the audience, he asked the old man what he thought of the speech.

"Well," the gentleman said thoughtfully, "I think for those who want to hear about those kinds of things, those were exactly the kinds of statements they wanted to hear."

◉⊙◎

Politician: "Do you know what made George Washington such a great president?"

Interviewer: "Sure, he never blamed any of the country's problems on the previous administration."

◉⊙◎

If every man were as true to his country as he is to his God, we'd be in a lot of trouble.

What food do detectives love?
Mystery meat.

⊙⊙⊙

A new bride cooked her first meal for her husband. "My mother taught me to cook, and I can cook two things well— apple pie and meatloaf."

The husband took a bite of his supper and asked, "And which one is this?"

⊙⊙⊙

Why was the mushroom the hit of the party?
He was a fungi.

I think that I shall never see
A hazard rougher than a tree;
A tree o'er which my ball must fly
If on the green it is to lie.

A tree which stands that green to guard,
And makes the shot extremely hard;
A tree whose leafy arms extend
To kill the six-iron shot I send.

A tree that stands in silence there,
While angry golfers rave and swear.
Irons were made for fools like me
Who cannot ever miss a tree.

—Author Unknown

◉ ⊙ ◎

Several chess enthusiasts checked into a hotel and were standing in the lobby, discussing their recent tournament victories. After an hour, the manager came out of the office and asked them to disperse.

"But why?" they asked as they moved off.

"Because," the manager explained, "I can't stand chess nuts boastin' in an open foyer."

◉ ⊙ ◎

If at first you don't succeed, skydiving is definitely not for you.

What's faster—hot or cold?
Hot is, because you can catch a cold.

⊙⊙⊚

I am cracked; I am made.
I am told; I am played.
What am I?
A joke.

⊙⊙⊚

How many men were born in 1920?
None. Only babies were born.

A four-year-old boy was asked to pray before dinner. The family members bowed their heads. The boy began his prayer, thanking God for all his friends and family members. Then he began to thank God for the food. He gave thanks for the chicken, the mashed potatoes, the fruit salad, and even the milk. Then he paused, and everyone waited.

After a long silence, the little boy opened one eye, looked at his mother, and whispered, "If I thank God for the broccoli, won't He know that I'm lying?"

◉⊙◎

Three fathers at a church meeting were talking about what they would do if a burglar broke into their houses at night.

"I'd call the police," said the first.

"I'd have my wife call the police while I grabbed the baseball bat," growled the second.

The third man, the father of three preschoolers, admitted, "If a burglar came into my room at night, I'd probably get up and take him to the bathroom."

◉⊙◎

When your teenage children have friends in distant cities, you become much more concerned about obscene phone bills than you are about obscene phone calls.

One morning a woman said to her husband, "I bet you don't know what day this is."

"Of course I do," he indignantly answered, going out the door on his way to the office.

At 11:00, the doorbell rang, and when the woman answered it, she was handed a box containing a dozen long-stemmed red roses.

At 1:00, a foil-wrapped box of her favorite chocolates arrived.

Later in the afternoon, a boutique delivered a designer dress.

The woman couldn't wait for her husband to come home. "First the flowers, then the candy, and then the dress!" she exclaimed when he walked in the door. "I've never had a more wonderful Groundhog Day in my whole life!"

◉ ◉ ◉

Lois: "You said you live off the *spat* of the land. Don't you mean the *fat* of the land?"
Glenn: "No, I'm a marriage counselor."

◉ ◉ ◉

Attending a wedding for the first time, a little girl whispered to her mother, "Why is the bride dressed in white?"

"Because white is the color of happiness," her mother explained, "and today is the happiest day in her life."

The child thought for a moment and then asked, "So why is the groom wearing black?"

What television channel do horses watch?
HayBC.

○○○

Fred: "Don't you wish life were like television?"
Ted: "I can't answer that now."
Fred: "Why not?"
Ted: "I'm on a commercial break."

○○○

What do you get if you cross MTV with flowerbeds?
Rock gardens.

Day
115

An American optometrist examined a Japanese national and reported bluntly, "You have a cataract."

"No, no," the patient corrected. "I drive a Rincoln Continentar."

◉◉◎

Patient: "Doc, what do you recommend for an insomniac like me?"

Doctor: "A good night's sleep."

◉◉◎

The doctor was trying to cheer Artie, who'd sprained his wrist. "When you get out of this sling," the doctor told him, "you'll feel better than ever. You'll be able to write, catch Frisbees, and bounce basketballs with the best of them."

Artie stopped crying and brightened up. "Wow!" he said. "I've never been able to bounce a basketball before!"

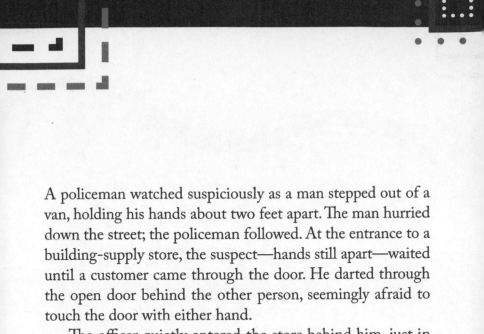

A policeman watched suspiciously as a man stepped out of a van, holding his hands about two feet apart. The man hurried down the street; the policeman followed. At the entrance to a building-supply store, the suspect—hands still apart—waited until a customer came through the door. He darted through the open door behind the other person, seemingly afraid to touch the door with either hand.

The officer quietly entered the store behind him, just in time to hear the suspect tell a clerk, "I need half a dozen three-by-fours cut exactly this long."

◉⊙◎

What do you call the police chief's wife?
Mischief.

◉⊙◎

Judge: "The last time I saw you, I told you I didn't want to ever see you again."

Defendant: "I told that to the policeman, but he didn't believe me."

What did the first arithmetic book say to the other arithmetic book?

I really have a lot of problems.

⊙⊙⊙

Maisy: "How's your son?"
Daisy: "Henry's at Harvard."
Maisy: "Really! What's he studying?"
Daisy: "Oh, he's not studying. They're studying him!"

⊙⊙⊙

Why is grammar a convict's least favorite subject?

He hates to complete the prison sentence.

Knock-knock
Who's there?
Descartes.
Descartes who?
Don't put Descartes before de horse.

⊙⊙⊚

Knock-knock.
Who's there?
Sonny and Cher.
Sonny and Cher who?
Sonny and Cher to be cloudy later.

⊙⊙⊚

Knock-knock.
Who's there?
Ptolemy.
Ptolemy who?
Ptolemy that you love me.

A "pillar of the church" passed away and was on his way to heaven. When he got to the pearly gates, he met an angel. The angel asked him what God's name was.

"Oh, that's easy," the man replied. "His name is Andy."

"What makes you think his name is Andy?" the angel asked.

"Well, you see, at church we used to sing this song: 'Andy walks with me, Andy talks with me.'"

◉◉◉

Top Seven Church Oxymorons:

7. Brief meeting
6. Pastor's day off
5. Early sign up
4. Clear calendar
3. Volunteer waiting list
2. Realistic budget
1. Concluding remarks

◉◉◉

At the close of the service, a visiting preacher remarked to the minister that he thought the singing was terribly poor and asked what the problem was. The home-team minister replied, "Yes, unfortunately the agnostics here are dreadful."

What did Delaware when Mississippi lent Missouri her New Jersey?
I don't know, Alaska.

⊙⊙⊙

Teacher: "Why is the Mississippi such an unusual river?"
Student: "Because it has four *I*s and can't see."

⊙⊙⊙

Why were the Indians the first people in North America?
They had reservations.

First octopus: "What do *you* like least about being an octopus?"
Second octopus: "Washing my hands before dinner."

⊙⊙⊙

Two hens were pecking in the yard when suddenly a softball came sailing over the fence, landing a few feet away from them. One hen said to the other, "Will you just look at the ones they're turning out next door!"

⊙⊙⊙

What happened to the leopard that took a bath three times a day?
After a week, he was spotless.

"Dad," a boy asked his father, "what's a *'necessary evil'*?"

"A necessary evil is one we like so much we don't want to abolish it, son."

◉◉◉

Milton Berle said that he practices an ancient martial art called Choo Dai Yuk: "When I'm attacked by an enemy, I scream. If that doesn't scare an attacker off, I go into my battle stance and kick, slash, and butt. If that doesn't take care of him, I go back to screaming."

◉◉◉

Al Kulwicki, stock car racer, on racing Saturday nights as opposed to Sunday afternoons: "It's basically the same, just darker."

Who was the first tennis player in the Bible?
Joseph. He served in Pharaoh's court.

⊙⊙⊙

You Might Be a Cross-Country Runner If. . .

Your shoes have more miles on them than your car does.
You need a magnifying glass to see your name in the paper.
You run farther in a week than your bus travels for meets.
The most enjoyable time you've had all month is a day off
    from practice.
You can spit and run at the same time.
You can eat your weight in spaghetti.
You schedule dates around meets.
Gatorade is your drug of choice.
Your Saturdays for the next four years are ruined.
You call bus seat 17 your second home.
Your dessert is brussels sprouts.

⊙⊙⊙

A baseball team scored four runs in one inning, but not one
man reached home. Why not?
It was a girl's team.

What do you get if you cross a skunk with a bear?
Winnie the Phew.

What does a bankrupt frog say?
"Baroke, baroke, baroke."

A woman has seven children; half of them are boys. How can this be possible?
All the children are boys, so half are boys and so is the other half.

Gabe: "Why are you down?"

Mike: "My sister said she wouldn't talk to me for two weeks."

Gabe: "Why should that upset you?"

Mike: "Today's the last day."

⊙⊙⊚

One morning a little boy proudly surprised his grandmother with a cup of coffee he had made himself. He anxiously waited to hear the verdict on the quality of the coffee. The grandmother had never in her life had such a bad cup of coffee, and as she forced down the last sip, she noticed three of those little green army guys in the bottom of the cup.

She asked, "Honey, why would three little green army guys be in the bottom of my cup?"

Her grandson replied, "You know, Grammy, it's just like on television. 'The best part of waking up is soldiers in your cup.'"

⊙⊙⊚

Two neighbors chatting by the fence noticed a third neighbor pacing up and down his driveway, a worried look on his face.

"What's the matter with Ed?" one asked.

"He's worried about his son," the other answered.

"Why? What's he got?"

"The BMW!"

Day
126

A rich suburbanite had car trouble while on a mountain holiday. He puttered into the yard of a rickety roadside filling station and called to the greasy, bearded attendant, "Have you had any experience with BMWs?"

"Buddy, if I could work on cars like that, I don't reckon I'd be here."

◉⊙◎

Maria: "What would you do if you were being chased by a runaway tractor-trailer truck at 70 miles an hour?"

Karl: "Eighty."

◉⊙◎

A lady went to an auto-parts store and asked for a seven-ten cap. All the clerks looked at each other, and one said, "What's a seven-ten cap?"

She said, "You know, it's right on the engine. Mine got lost somehow and I need a new one."

"What kind of a car is it on?" the clerk asked.

"My 2000 Toyota," she replied.

"Well, how big is it?"

She made a circle with her hands about three-and-a-half inches in diameter.

The clerk asked, "What does it do?"

"I don't know, but it's always been there."

At this point, the manager came over. He handed her a notepad and asked her if she could draw a picture of it. The customer carefully drew a circle about three-and-a-half inches in diameter. In the center she writes, "710."

The manager, looking at the drawing upside down, walked to a shelf and grabbed an OIL cap.

An optometrist examining an elderly patient asked, "Can you read the fifth line on the chart?"

"No."

"How about the fourth line?"

"No."

"Hmm. Try the second line."

"I can't read that one, either."

"Surely you can read the first line."

"Truth is, I've never learned to read."

◉◉◎

The struggling young pediatrician put up the following sign beside his office door: SMALL FEVERS GRATEFULLY RECEIVED.

◉◉◎

Dentist's hymn: "Crown Him With Many Crowns"
Psychiatrist's hymn: "Just a Little Talk With Jesus"
Paramedic's hymn: "Revive Us Again"

A police officer was escorting a prisoner to jail when the officer's hat blew off down the sidewalk.

"Would you like me to get that for you?" asked the prisoner.

"You must think I'm an idiot!" said the officer. "You just wait here, and I'll get it."

⊙⊙⊙

A criminal said to the judge, "Your Honor, I'm not guilty. I know I can prove it if you'll just give me some time."

"Sure," replied the judge. "Ten years. Next!"

⊙⊙⊙

Did you hear about the crimes over at that house they're renovating? The shower was stalled while the curtains were held up. Apparently the doors were also hung, and I heard the window was framed for it.

Have you heard about the new magazine in the library for athletic dogs? It's called *Spots Illustrated*.

⊙⊙⊙

Teacher: "Define *'absolute zero.'*"
Greg: "The lowest grade you can get on a test."

⊙⊙⊙

What is the butterfly's favorite class?
Moth-ematics.

Day 130

Knock-knock.
Who's there?
Picasso.
Picasso who?
"Picasso you, there's a song in my heart."

⦿⦿⦿

Knock-knock.
Who's there?
Wilbur Wright.
Wilbur Wright who?
Wilbur Wright back after these commercials.

⦿⦿⦿

Knock-knock.
Who's there?
Abraham Lincoln.
Abraham Lincoln who?
Come on now, there's only one Abraham Lincoln.

A candidate and his wife fell into the hotel bed at the end of a long day on the campaign trail.

"I'm exhausted," groaned the wife.

"I think I have more right to be exhausted than you do," complained the candidate. "I delivered six speeches in six no-account little towns today."

"And I had to listen to the same message six times."

◉◉◉

What are the three great American parties?
Democratic, Republican, and Tupperware.

◉◉◉

What was the first thing Queen Elizabeth did upon ascending the throne?
She sat down.

Why can't you play hide-and-seek with poultry in a Chinese restaurant?
Because of the Peking duck.

◉◉◉

First fish: "I've been in schools all my life."
Second fish: "Really think you're smart, don't you? Listen, you may be educated, but my ancestors swam under the *Mayflower*."

◉◉◉

What is a shark's favorite game?
Swallow the Leader.

Reporter: "Do you like your job, sir?"
Astronomer: "Yes. It's heavenly."

⊙⊙⊙

"Dad, I want to be a salesman like you when I grow up."

"Oh, no. Sales are tough these days. You'll have a much better future in technology."

"But I think I'll have a great future in sales."

"Nope. The future's not what it used to be."

⊙⊙⊙

What sign does a nuclear scientist post on the office door when he leaves for vacation?

GONE FISSION.

Day 134

Mr. Elf: "I watch a lot of television."
Mr. Hobbit: "What's your favorite kind of program?"
Mr. Elf: "Gnome improvement shows."

⊙⊙⊙

What did Cinderella call the cat who helped her get to the ball?
"My furry godmother."

⊙⊙⊙

Knock-knock.
Who's there?
Ron.
Ron who?
Ron, Ron, Ron as fast as you can—you can't catch me, I'm the gingerbread man!

Lawyer to defendant: "Do you wish to challenge any of the jury members?"
Defendant: "Well, I think I could take that guy on the end."

◉ ◉ ◉

A lawyer and his doctor friend were working out at the gym.

"I come here to exercise, but people are always asking me for advice," the doctor complained to the lawyer. "What do you think I should do?"

"Well," said the lawyer, "the next time you give advice, send a bill."

A few days later, the doctor opened his mail and found a bill—from the lawyer.

◉ ◉ ◉

Judge: "You have been accused of hitting a comedian with your car, then dragging him four blocks."
Driver: "It was only three blocks, Your Honor."
Judge: "That's still carrying a joke too far."

Church Signs:

"Free Trip to Heaven. Details Inside."

"Try Our Sundays. They Are Better Than Baskin-Robbins."

"People Are Like Tea Bags—You Have to Put Them in Hot Water before You Know How Strong They Are."

"Running Low on Faith? Stop in for a Fill-up."

"If You Can't Sleep, Don't Count Sheep. Talk to the Shepherd."

"No God—No Peace. Know God—Know Peace."

"God So Loved the World That He Did Not Send a Committee."

"Fight Truth Decay—Read the Bible!"

"If You're Headed in the Wrong Direction, God Allows for U-turns."

"If You Don't Like the Way You Were Born, Try Being Born Again."

◉⊙◎

I don't mind going to a church service in a drive-in theatre. But when they hold the baptisms in a car wash, that's going too far.

◉⊙◎

Miss Gladys was a regular fixture in morning worship at First Church. On this one particular morning, the pastor's message went on forever. Some in the congregation dozed off.

Following the service, she walked up to a very sleepy-looking visitor to welcome him. "Hello, I'm Gladys Dunn."

To which the visitor replied, "You're not the only one."

What would you give an absentminded squirrel?
Forget-me-nuts.

◉◉◉

"Have you got any kittens going cheap?" asked a customer in a pet shop.

"No, sir," replied the owner. "All our kittens go, *'Meow.'*"

◉◉◉

A hungry lion was roaming through the jungle, looking for something to eat. He came across two men. One was sitting under a tree, reading a book; the other was typing away on his laptop. The lion quickly pounced on the man reading the book and devoured him.

Even the king of the jungle knows that readers digest, and writers cramp.

Silence can be an excellent substitute for brilliance.

⊚⊙⊚

It was Will Rogers who pointed out that getting yourself on the right track in life is only half the task. You'll get run over anyway if you stand still.

⊚⊙⊚

An anonymous New Orleans general manager, after a loss, was asked what he thought of the refs: "I'm not allowed to comment on lousy officiating."

Murphy's Laws of Spectator Sports: Exciting plays occur only while you are watching the scoreboard or out buying garlic fries.

○○○

A father and son were watching a basketball game on television. The father was getting more and more upset as a player on the team he supported kept giving away fouls.

"What an idiot," he shouted. "What on earth is he doing playing in such an important game?"

His son sat quietly for a while, then said, "Daddy, maybe it's his ball."

○○○

What is a prizefighter's favorite drink?
Punch.

What is an owl's favorite mystery?
A whooo-dunit.

⊙⊙⊙

Molly left a solid object on the kitchen counter while she went to play. When she came back four hours later, the object had completely vanished. No one touched it or ate it. What happened?
Molly left an ice cube on the counter.

⊙⊙⊙

What do you call a story told by a giraffe?
A tall tale.

It was bedtime for Timmy and Jimmy, who were staying overnight with their grandparents. While kneeling to say his prayers, Timmy began praying at the top of his lungs, "Dear God, for Christmas I want some video games, a motor bike, a DVD player. . ."

"Whoa!" Jimmy hollered, "Why are you yelling? God isn't deaf."

"I know God's not deaf," replied Timmy. "But Grandma is!"

Mother: "Kids, what are you arguing about?"
David: "Oh, there isn't any argument. Lisa thinks I'm not going to give her half of my candy, and I think the same thing."

"Do you get spanked much?" a child asked his friend.

"Yes. I think I'm the kind of boy my parents don't want me to play with."

Ruth: "I heard your husband isn't taking you on vacation to Cancun this summer after all. Is it true?"

Emily: "No. It's Paris he's not taking me to this summer. Cancun is where we didn't go last summer."

⊙⊙⊙

A tourist in the Middle East was having a hard time shaking off a street hawker who wanted to sell him the "genuine skull of Genghis Khan."

"You're asking far too much, and I don't have luggage space to carry it home. Besides, it's repulsive—and I don't believe it's authentic."

The street seller reached into his bag and came up with a smaller skull, equally gross. He smiled broadly. "Half price—but *eenfeeneetlee* more valuable: skull of the great Khan, age twelve."

⊙⊙⊙

Midge: "How did you like Venice?"

Esther: "It was dreadful. The streets were flooded the entire time we were there."

Chuck: "My doctor said I had to give up playing the drums."
Cluck: "Why?"
Chuck: "He lives in the apartment below me."

⊙⊙⊙

Definitions:

Practical Nurse: A nurse who marries a wealthy patient.
Specialist: A doctor who prefers a smaller practice and a larger house.
Psychiatry: One profession in which the customer is always wrong.

⊙⊙⊙

Sydney: "I must have sneezed fifty times today. Do you think there's something in the air?"
Allen: "Yes—your germs!"

"They were causing an awful lot of commotion at the zoo, Your Honor," the zoo attendant said.

"Boys," said the judge sternly, "I never like to hear reports of juvenile delinquency. Now I want each of you to tell me your name and what you were doing wrong."

"My name is George," said the first boy, "and I threw peanuts into the elephant pen."

"My name is Larry," said the second boy, "and I threw peanuts into the elephant pen."

"My name is Mike," said the third boy, "and I threw peanuts into the elephant pen."

"My name is Peanuts," said the fourth boy.

⊙⊙⊙

Why did the dermatologist hurry to the jail?
Everyone was breaking out.

⊙⊙⊙

A police officer saw a lady driving and knitting at the same time, so after driving next to her for a while, he yelled, "Pull over!"

"No!" she called back. "It's a pair of socks!"

Sally: "How did you pass the entrance exam for candy-making school?"
Rita: "It was simple. I fudged it."

What kind of tests are dental students good at?
True or floss.

What did the meteorology student say about his final exam?
"It was a breeze with only a few foggy patches."

Knock-knock.
Who's there?
Adolph.
Adolph who?
Adolph ball hit me on the head.

◉ ⊙ ◎

Knock-knock.
Who's there?
Zeus.
Zeus who?
Zeus house is this anyway?

◉ ⊙ ◎

Knock-knock.
Who's there?
Deduct.
Deduct who?
Donald deduct.

Chris: "Did you hear about the computer that went to the doctor complaining of a chronic cough?"
Pam: "No. What was the diagnosis?"
Chris: "It had come down with a virus."

◉◉◉

Rachel: "Do you know the difference between Daddy's toys and our brother's toys?"
Fran: "Yeah, Daddy's cost a lot more money."

◉◉◉

Which way did the programmer go?
He went data way.

Which U.S. President liked to clean house?
Hoover.

◉⊙◎

Knock-knock.
Who's there?
Eisenhower.
Eisenhower who?
Eisenhower late for school.

◉⊙◎

What did the flag say to Thomas Jefferson?
Nothing. It just waved.

You Know You're from California When...

The fastest part of your commute is down your driveway.
You were born somewhere else.
You know how to eat an artichoke.
You go to a tanning salon before you hit the beach.
You drive to your neighborhood block party.

⊙⊙⊙

Why are you always welcome in the Show-Me-State?
Because Missouri loves company.

⊙⊙⊙

Late one hot morning, two northern tourists driving through Louisiana saw on the map the next logical stop for lunch would be a town called Natchitoches. They wondered about the pronunciation, one favoring NATCH-ee-toe-cheese and the other saying it made more sense as Natch-eye-TOTT-chez.

They stopped at a fast-food joint and went inside. A fresh-faced girl took their order. One tourist said, "We need somebody local to settle an argument for us. Could you please pronounce where we are...very slowly?"

The girl leaned over the counter so they could watch her lips and said as distinctly as she could, "Brrrr, grrrr, Kiinnnggg."

When Sleeping Beauty got lost in the castle gardens, how did she feel?

A-maze-d.

⊙⊙⊙

Exasperated dragon on the field of battle: "Mother said there would be knights like this."

⊙⊙⊙

Medieval History According to Students:

In the Middle Ages, King Alfred conquered the Dames.

King Arthur lived in the Age of Shivery; King Harold mustarded his troops before the Battle of Hastings; and Joan of Arc was canonized by Bernard Shaw.

The Magna Carta provided that no free man should be hanged twice for the same offense.

In medieval times, most of the people were alliterate. The greatest writer of the time was Chaucer, who wrote many poems and versus and also wrote literature. Another tale tells of William Tell, who shot an arrow through an apple while standing on his son's head.

An anonymous letter writer sent his letter to the local newspaper editor, complaining that church attendance made no sense. "I've gone for thirty years," he wrote, "and have heard something like three thousand sermons. But for the life of me, I can't remember a single one of them. So I think I'm wasting my time, as are the preachers for even bothering to deliver a sermon at all."

This letter started a real controversy on the op-ed page. It went on for weeks until someone wrote this clincher:

"I've been married for thirty years. In that time my wife has cooked some thirty-two thousand meals, but for the life of me, I can recall the menu of few, if any, of those meals. I do know, though, they all nourished me and gave me the strength I need to do my work. If my wife had not given me those meals, I'd be dead today."

No more comments about sermon contents have appeared on the op-ed page.

◉◉◉

When you call a dog, he usually comes to you. When you call a cat, he takes a message.

◉◉◉

"Look at that speed!" said one hawk to another as a jet-fighter plane zoomed over their heads.

"Hmph!" snorted the other. "You would fly fast, too, if your tail was on fire!"

It's said that absence makes the heart grow fonder. If that is so, a huge bunch of people sure love their church.

⊙⊙⊙

Were it not for the last minute, few things would be done on time.

⊙⊙⊙

A man brought his dog to a veterinarian's office. The animal was quite stiff and seemed, to all appearances, dead. But the man wanted to make sure.

So the vet examined the corpse thoroughly and pronounced with certainty that the dog had indeed passed away. The man, very upset, asked, "Is there nothing at all you can do? I have to be absolutely certain little Morty is gone before I can begin to deal with it and find peace."

The vet thought a moment, then whispered to an assistant, who went into another room and returned momentarily with a live cat. The cat was placed on the table beside the dog and sniffed the corpse from one end to the other. Then it hopped down from the table and walked back into the other room.

"No question whatsoever," the veterinarian said. "Morty is dead."

The vet then wrote out a bill for 200 dollars.

"I don't understand," the man said in dismay. "You're charging me 200 dollars to verify the death of my dog?"

"Not exactly," the vet explained. "My examination was 50 fifty. The other 150 dollars is for the cat scan."

Harvey: "Who was the greatest female financier in the Bible?"
Midge: "Pharaoh's daughter. She went down to the bank of the Nile and drew out a little prophet."

○⊙◎

"Inflation is creeping up," a young man said to his friend. "Yesterday I ordered a twenty-five-dollar steak in a restaurant and told them to put it on my credit card—and it fit."

○⊙◎

Have you seen the little fifty-page best seller called *Money Isn't Everything*? It costs $29.95.

Boxing promoter Dan Duva on Mike Tyson hooking up again with promoter Don King: "Why would anyone expect him to come out smarter? He went to prison for three years, not Princeton."

⊙⊙⊙

A church bulletin item announcing a covered dish supper concluded: "Prayer and medication to follow."

⊙⊙⊙

More Church Signs:

"The Best Vitamin for a Christian is B1."
"Soul Food Served Here."
"Beat the Christmas Rush, Come to Church This Sunday."
"Don't Give Up. Moses Was Once a Basket Case!"
"To Belittle Is to Be Little."
"So Live That No Matter What Happens, It Wouldn't Happen to a Nicer Person."
"After Two Thousand Years, We Are Still under the Same Management."
"It Is Unlikely There'll Be a Reduction in the Wages of Sin."

Whenever I go to a ball game, I always end up in the same seat—between the hot dog vendor and his best customer.

◉◉◎

What do you call basketball goals in Hawaii?
Hula hoops.

◉◉◎

Did you hear about the Olympic swimmer who sank all of his money into a swimming pool company and went bankrupt? He got in way over his head.

What is a frog's favorite flower?
A croakus.

◉ ◉ ◉

What has twelve legs, six eyes, three tails, and cannot see?
Three blind mice.

◉ ◉ ◉

"I guarantee," said the salesman in the pet shop, "that this parrot will repeat every word it hears." A customer bought the bird but found that the parrot wouldn't speak a single word. However, the salesman didn't lie about the bird. How is this possible?
The parrot was deaf.

Alice: "Grandpa, were you on Noah's ark?"
Grandpa: "Oh, no."
Alice: "Then how did you survive the flood?"

◉◉◉

"Where are your ice skates?" Dad asked.

Laurence replied, "I let Molly use them."

"That was very nice of you. Where is she now?"

"She's out on the lake, checking to see if the ice is thick enough."

◉◉◉

Why did Adam get the first fig leaf?
Because he wore the plants in the family.

A teacher asked, "Who was the first brother to fly an airplane at Kitty Hawk, North Carolina? Was it Orville or Wilbur?"

"Orville!" shouted one student.

"Wilbur!" shouted another.

"They're both Wright," said a third.

◉ ⊙ ◉

Bumper Stickers:

EVACUATE THE ROAD—STUDENT DRIVING.
HUG YOUR KIDS AT HOME AND BELT THEM IN THE CAR.
TRUST IN GOD—BUT LOCK YOUR CAR.
CAUTION! DRIVER APPLYING MAKEUP.

◉ ⊙ ◉

Two truck drivers came to a low bridge. The clearance sign said ten feet eight inches. When they got out and measured their truck, they discovered their vehicle was eleven feet. The first man looked at the other and said, "I can't see any cops around. Let's go for it!"

They're a perfect match: He's a chiropractor, and she's a pain in the neck.

◉◉◉

A Limerick

There once was a lady name Lynn
Who was so uncommonly thin,
That when she assayed
To drink lemonade,
She slipped through the straw and fell in.

◉◉◉

Lilly: "I just finished a three-month diet."
Jenny: "What did you lose?"
Lilly: "Three months of good eating."

Prosecutor: "How far away from the scene of the crime were you when you heard the first shot?"

Witness: "About thirty feet."

Prosecutor: "How far away were you when the second shot was fired?"

Witness: "About two hundred yards."

⊙⊙⊚

When the detective got to the crime scene, how did he know that the numbers were guilty?

Their alibi didn't add up.

⊙⊙⊚

"Why didn't you report this robbery when you arrived home at midmorning?" the investigating officer asked the housewife.

"I wasn't sure it was a robbery. I thought at first my husband had simply been looking for his neckties."

Teacher: "I would like to go through one whole day without having to tell you to behave."
Student: "You have my permission."

⊙⊙⊙

Playing hooky is like a credit card—fun now, pay later.

⊙⊙⊙

Drew and Luis were late for their English Lit final exam. Thinking quickly, they rubbed some dirt and grease on their face and hands and agreed on an excuse. By the time they got to the room, the other students had already completed their exams and left.

"We're so sorry, Professor Morris," said Drew, "but on the way here, we got a flat tire, and Luis and I had to change it ourselves."

"Come back tomorrow," said Professor Morris, smiling. "I'll let you make it up then."

Drew and Luis were happy with the reprieve and spent the rest of the day playing outdoors.

The following morning, they arrived on time to complete the exam. The professor put the young men in separate rooms. The students found that there was only one question on the final exam. It read simply, "Which tire?"

Knock-knock.
Who's there?
Thermos.
Thermos who?
Thermos be a doorbell here some place.

⊙⊙⊙

Knock-knock.
Who's there?
Orson.
Orson who?
Orson wagon are parked outside.

⊙⊙⊙

Knock-knock.
Who's there?
Punch!
Punch who?
Not me! I just got here!

Kirstie: "Why does your father go to work at the bakery?"
Allie: "He kneads the dough."

⊙⊙⊙

Why did the weather announcer quit her job?
She didn't find the weather very agreeable.

⊙⊙⊙

Tim: "What do you do for a living?"
Jim: "I work with figures."
Tim: "Accountant?"
Jim: "No. Fitness instructor."

Teacher: "Who succeeded the first president of the United States?"

Student: "The second one."

◉◉◎

Where are the kings and queens of England crowned?
On their heads.

◉◉◎

"Is it true that President Lincoln wrote the Gettysburg Address while riding from Washington to the battleground on the back of an envelope?" a student asked.

"Yes, that's what the history books tell us," replied the teacher.

"How many legs did the envelope have?"

Gambler 1: "I finally found a foolproof way to come back from Las Vegas with a small fortune."

Gambler 2: "Tell me—quick!"

Gambler 1: "Go there with a large fortune."

◉☉◉

Rudy: "Does money really talk?"

Judy: "It does to me. Every time I go to the mall my cash says, 'Good buy! Good buy!'"

◉☉◉

It was a conservative and boring economist who was lecturing to a college class when he saw that one of his students had fallen asleep. Making a fist, the economist pounded on the table, which in turn awoke the startled student, who responded, "Cut taxes and reduce government spending."

Santa Claus was confused when he found three red-nosed reindeer as he prepared his sleigh. "What's this?" he asked Mrs. Claus. "Which one is Rudolph?"

Mrs. Claus wiped the noses of the three reindeer with her apron. Amazingly, only one red-nosed reindeer—the true Rudolph—remained.

"It's no real mystery," she explained. "Dancer and Prancer have been eating my cherry cobbler again."

⊙⊙⊙

Definition:

Super Bowl: Swimming pool for Superman's goldfish.

⊙⊙⊙

Knock-knock.
Who's there?
E. T.
E. T. who?
E. T. your food before it gets cold.

A church is an excellent place to go for faithlifts.

◉◉◉

The following is a report on some ministerial candidates:

Noah: Prone to unrealistic building projects.

Joseph: A big thinker, but a bit of a braggart. Believes in dream interpreting, has a prison record, and has been accused of adultery.

David: The most promising candidate of all until our discovery of affair with his neighbor's wife. His kids are out of control, and he's a proponent of upbeat musical expressions.

Solomon: Great preacher, but our parsonage would never hold all those wives. Good with building projects, but rather extravagant.

Jonah: Ran away from God's call. Known to pout when things don't go his way. Tells questionable fish stories.

John: Says he's a Baptist but doesn't dress like one. Has a weird diet. Offends politicians and is known to lose his head.

Jesus: Seldom stays in one place very long. He's single. Some say he has a Messiah complex.

Peter: Too blue-collar. Has a bad temper. Claims to have visions.

Paul: Powerful CEO-type leader. Considered short on tact, unforgiving with younger ministers, seemingly harsh, and has been known to preach all night. Controversial on women's issues. Little chance that he'll ever marry.

Judas: His references are solid. Conservative and pragmatic. Good connections. Knows how to handle money. We're inviting him to preach next Sunday. Possibilities here.

◉◉◉

Where do wasps live?
Stingapore.

**Day
168**

Church Nursery Sign:

1 Corinthians 15:51: "We Shall Not All Sleep, but We Shall Be Changed."

◉◉◉

A pastor and a deacon visited a house to call on a parishioner.

They knocked, and a small voice replied, "Come in."

They went in, but although they found no one there, they did find two big Doberman dogs poised to attack them.

They said, "Hello, is anyone here?" and the voice of a little old lady said, "Come in."

It sounded like it was coming from the kitchen, so they went in that direction. They came upon a parrot, which was repeatedly saying, "Come in, come in, come in. . ."

The pastor said, "You silly old parrot, is that all you can say?"

With the same small voice, the parrot said, "Sic 'em."

◉◉◉

What time is it when five grizzly bears are chasing you?
Five after one.

"Smoking," commented author Fletcher Knebel, "is one of the leading causes of statistics."

⊙⊙⊙

You asked me why I liked professional sports. . . . Where else can I boo a bunch of millionaires to their faces?

⊙⊙⊙

Humorous Headlines:

SHORTAGE OF BRAINS HAMPERS RESEARCH
BUS STRIKES MAN, DECLINES ASSISTANCE
AIRPLANE HITS THREE HOUSES, KILLS TWO
SUSPECT WOUNDS WRONG WIFE, SAYS HE'S SORRY

Two well-heeled ladies flying first-class condescended, after an hour of silent boredom, to strike up a conversation with each other.

"I just had a delightful note from my son the surgeon," intoned one. "Do you have children?"

"My only son lives in New York."

"And what does he do?"

"He, too, has chosen to pursue the medical profession."

"Lovely. I suppose he's a GP."

"He's a malpractice lawyer."

⊙⊙⊙

Lawyer to witness: "Mr. Roper, how did your first marriage end?"

Witness: "It ended in death."

Lawyer: "The death of your spouse?"

⊙⊙⊙

Another lawyer, posing a similarly inane question to a witness, caught himself in the middle of it, broke off, and besought the judge: "Your Honor, I would like to withdraw the next question."

"Just think of it," said the braggart boxer to his manager. "Tonight I'll be fighting on television before millions of people."

"Yes," replied the weary manager, "and they'll all know the results of the fight at least ten seconds before you do."

◉◉◉

John: "How is music like ice skating?"
Jen: "If you don't 'C-sharp,' you'll 'B-flat'."

◉◉◉

A Skier's Glossary:

Alp: One of a number of ski mountains in Europe. Also a request for help.

Avalanche: An actual peril skiers face. See also: *Blizzard, Death on the Slopes, First Aid, Fracture, Frostbite, Hypothermia, Lift Collapse.*

Bindings: Automatic mechanisms that protect skiers from serious injuries during a fall by releasing skis from boots, sending the skis skittering across the slope where they can trip two other skiers.

Gravity: One of the fundamental forces of nature that affects skiers. The other three are the strong force that makes bindings jam; the weak force that makes ankles give way on turns; and electromagnetism, that produces dead batteries in expensive ski-resort parking lots.

Skier: One who pays an arm and a leg for the opportunity to break them.

Traverse: To ski across a slope at an angle. One of two quick and simple methods of reducing speed.

Tree: The other method.

You hope you never have it. But when you do, you hope you never lose it. What is it?

A lawsuit.

⊙⊙⊙

Two fathers and two sons went duck hunting. Each shot a duck, but they shot only three ducks in all. How come?

The hunters were a man, his son, and his grandson.

⊙⊙⊙

A woman shoots her husband. Then she holds him underwater for over five minutes.

Finally, she hangs him. But one hour later they both go out together and enjoy a wonderful dinner. How is this possible?

The woman was a photographer. She shot a picture of her husband, developed it, and hung it up to dry.

Kendra: "Martin, what will you do when you grow up to be as big as your daddy?"
Martin: "Go on a diet, first of all."

◉◉◎

"My grandmother is always complaining about how awful it feels to be old," Carmen said.

"Mine, too," said Dixie. "I guess those wrinkles hurt a lot."

◉◉◎

After a lesson on weather in the month of March, the teacher asked her class, "What is it that comes in like a lion and goes out like a lamb?"

A student answered, "My dad."

Day 174

"I wish I had enough money to buy a Rolls-Royce," John said.

"Why do you want a Rolls-Royce?" asked Andrew.

"I don't. It's the money I want."

⊙⊙⊙

Why did the tire get fired from its job?
It couldn't stand the pressure.

⊙⊙⊙

Bill: "Did you tell Stan the new airplane joke?"
Phil: "Yeah, but I think it went right over his head."

What did the doctor do when he discovered the weight machine had been stolen from the nurse's office?
He launched a full-scale investigation.

⊙⊙⊙

Patient: "Doctor! Something's wrong! I'm shrinking!"
Doctor: "Take it easy, sir. You'll just have to be a little patient."

⊙⊙⊙

Why was Humpty Dumpty referred to a psychiatrist?
He had cracked up.

Day 176

A policeman was interrogating two suspects. "Where do you live?" he asked the first.

"No permanent address."

"What about you?" the policeman asked the second.

"Next door to him."

⊙⊙⊙

Did you hear about the two hundred stolen mattresses? Police are springing into action to find the criminals.

⊙⊙⊙

Two prisoners were commiserating. "What are you in here for?" asked one.

"Stealing a truckload of cement."

"Catch you red-handed?"

"Yeah, the evidence was pretty concrete."

Teacher: "Felix, when is the boiling point reached?"
Felix: "Just after my father reads my report card."

⊙⊙⊙

Where is the best place to have the nurse's office at school?
Next to the cafeteria.

⊙⊙⊙

"If you have ten pieces of bubble gum and you give away four, what do you have then?" the teacher asked.

"I have six pieces of gum and four new friends!" replied the student.

Knock-knock
Who's there?
Yachts.
Yachts who?
"Yachts new, pussycat?"

⊙⊙⊚

Knock-knock.
Who's there?
Utah.
Utah who?
Utah the puddy cat, too?

⊙⊙⊚

Knock-knock.
Who's there?
Izzy.
Izzy who?
Izzy come, Izzy go.

A Greek tailor in Chicago had a lighthearted routine for customers who brought in torn dress coats or pants for repair.

"Euripides?" he would ask.

To which knowing regulars would respond, "That's right. Eumenides?"

◉⊙◎

A boss ended the day with instructions to the secretary for tomorrow:

"I've just finished dictating about forty letters; type them up and get them in the mail. You also need to go to the office-supply store and take notes on those three new fax/printer models so we can choose one and get the purchase approved right away. Barnes is coming in at 2:00, and she'll want you to go through the new shipping contracts with her—but get her out of here by 3:30 so you can take notes at the staff meeting. Oh, Wilkins wants you to have the contact database updated and distributed before the meeting—and please type up my committee report; I'll try to have it dictated by late morning. And don't forget to show Abercrombie how to key in the title insurance information on the new forms. Think you can manage all that?"

"Sure," said the secretary, not batting an eye. "I'll bring my television set, in case I get bored."

◉⊙◎

Farmer Brown: "Did you lose much in that last tornado?"
Farmer Jones: "Lost the henhouse and all the chickens. But that was all right—I ended up with three new cows and somebody's pickup truck."

Day 180

Who was the least favorite president of chickens?
Herbert Hoover, the man who promised "A chicken in every pot."

◉ ◉ ◉

One candidate at a political rally held the podium a full forty minutes with what had to be the most meaningless, boring speech in the county's history. Finally, he concluded and asked if anyone in the audience had a question.

"I do," piped up a voice. "Who's your opponent?"

◉ ◉ ◉

"I see old Senator Jones isn't quite as big a windbag as he used to be," said Elliott after a political rally.

"You think he's mellower these days?"

"Oh, no, but he's lost a little weight."

Driver: "Does this road lead to Prairie Village?"
Kansan: "Don't know."
Driver: "Well, can you tell me which road I should take to get to Johnson County?"
Kansan: "Nope."
Driver: "You sure don't know much, do you?"
Kansan: "Maybe not. But I'm not the guy who's lost!"

⊙⊙⊙

A rancher was gazing across the vast expanse of the Grand Canyon for the first time in his life. "That," he remarked, "would be a mighty tough place to recover stray cattle."

⊙⊙⊙

What do you get if you cross a native of Maine with a cartoonist?
A Yankee Doodler.

What fishing technique do the Three Billy Goats Gruff use?
Trolling.

⊙⊙⊙

There was this knight who was very brave but a little odd. While all the other knights rode horses, he preferred to ride his faithful Great Dane.

One night, while returning from a trip, he was caught in a downpour and sought shelter at an inn. The innkeeper did not like knights and refused to give him a room. But when he saw the dog standing there soaking wet, his heart softened.

"I couldn't turn a knight out on a dog like this," he said.

⊙⊙⊙

Why did Little Miss Muffet need directions?
She had lost her whey.

Teacher: "In 1940, what were the Poles doing in Russia?"
Student: "Holding up the telegraph lines."

◉◉◉

What did Napoleon become after his thirty-ninth birthday?
Forty years old.

◉◉◉

Hilary: "When did Caesar utter the famous statement, 'Et tu, Brute?'"
Sam: "When Brutus asked him how many cheeseburgers he'd had at the cookout."

A little girl was sitting in church with her father when she suddenly felt ill. "Daddy," she whispered, "I have to frow up!" Her father told her to hurry to the restroom.

In less than two minutes the child was back. "I didn't have to go too far," she explained. "There's a box by the front door with a sign that says, 'FOR THE SICK.'"

⊙⊙⊙

Too many Christians want to serve the Lord in advisory roles.

⊙⊙⊙

One balmy evening in the South Pacific, a navy ship spied smoke coming from one of three huts on an uncharted island.

Upon arriving at the shore, the crew was met by a shipwreck survivor. He said, "I'm so glad you're here. I've been alone on this island for more than five years."

The captain replied, "If you're all alone, why do I see three huts?"

The survivor answered, "Well, I live in one and go to church in another."

"What about the third hut?" asked the captain.

"That's where I used to go to church."

One morning a man telephoned his neighbor at four o'clock in the morning and said, "Your dog is barking and keeping me awake."

The neighbor called him back at four o'clock the next morning and said, "I don't have a dog."

◉ ◉ ◎

Show me an owl with laryngitis, and I'll show you a bird that doesn't give a hoot.

◉ ◉ ◎

What do ducks like on television?
Duckumentaries.

"I just heard of an Alaskan who wants to visit Texas, but he's afraid to. Suffers from claustrophobia."

◉ ⊙ ◎

When antique dealers get together, how do they strike up a conversation? Does one of them venture, "What's new?"

◉ ⊙ ◎

A newspaper ran a blistering editorial in which it stated, "We believe half the members of city council are swindlers."

City hall and its political supporters flooded the editor's phone line for three days. Finally, a retraction was promised. It read: "We now believe half the members of city council are not swindlers."

A group of baseball players were commiserating after a game. "Can you believe it?" one player said to the others. "We paid the ump one hundred dollars in advance to give us the game, and he let us lose anyway."

"Some umpires are thieves," consoled his friends.

$$\odot\odot\odot$$

If one synchronized swimmer drowns, do the rest have to drown, too?

$$\odot\odot\odot$$

Ernie and Bernie put on their ice skates and ventured out onto the frozen lake. After skating in circles for a while, Ernie stopped and asked Bernie, "Do you think there are any ducks around here?"

"Of course not," answered Bernie. "They all flew south for the winter."

"Well, in that case," replied Ernie in a panicky voice, "I think the ice is quacking!"

What is cut and spread out on the table but never eaten?
A deck of cards.

◉ ⊙ ◎

A horse is tied to a four-foot rope, and five feet away is a bail of hay. Without breaking the rope or chewing through it, the horse was able to get to the bail of hay. How is this possible?
The other end of the rope wasn't tied to anything.

◉ ⊙ ◎

Which bird is always out of breath?
A puffin.

A lonesome woman parishioner demanded a home visit from her pastor. So, as promised, the reverend showed up and sat by the woman's bed, listening to her litany of woe. Finally he asked to read some passages from her Bible.

In a much-too-sweet voice, she called to her little daughter playing in the next room, "Darling, please bring Mother that dear old book that she reads every night."

Promptly the little girl brought in a copy of a popular television-movie magazine.

◉ ◉ ◉

What's the best way to keep children from overhearing what you're saying?
Say it to them.

◉ ◉ ◉

A couple returned home from a party at about 2:00 a.m. and noticed their neighbor pacing back and forth on his darkened front porch.

"Can we help you?" they called across the yard.

"No," he said huffily. "I forgot my keys, and I've been waiting for my teenaged daughter to come home and unlock the door."

NASA scientists have an ingenious way of determining whether a distant planet is inhabited. They program the landing craft to mechanically dig a hole in the surface. If no one comes to stand around and watch, they know the planet is void of life.

◉ ⊙ ◎

How long is a computer's attention span?
As long as its power cord.

◉ ⊙ ◎

Max thought it was cool being the son of a noted computer programmer until he came home from school one day, sacked out in front of the television set like always, and saw this stream across the screen: WE INTERRUPT THIS PROGRAM BECAUSE WE HAVE SERIOUS REASON TO BELIEVE YOU HAVEN'T DONE YOUR HOMEWORK.

The University of Alabama football team played Harvard. At a party after the game, an Alabama player approached a girl and asked, "What school do you go to?"

"Yale," the girl replied.

"Okay, *WHAT SCHOOL DO YOU GO TO?*"

⊙⊙⊙

A Texan was trying to impress a guy from Boston with a graphic account of the heroism at the Alamo. He says, "I guess you don't have many heroes where you come from?"

The man from Boston replies, "Well, sir, have you ever heard of Paul Revere?"

And the Texan says, "Paul Revere? Isn't he the guy who ran for help?"

⊙⊙⊙

An Alaskan was on trial in Anchorage. The judge turned to him and asked, "Where were you on the night of October to April?"

A group of kindergarteners was on a class outing to its local police station where the kids saw pictures, tacked to a bulletin board, of the ten most-wanted men.

One of the youngsters pointed to a picture and asked if it really was the photo of a wanted person.

"Yes," answered the policeman.

"Well," wondered the child, "why didn't you keep him when you took his picture?"

⊙⊙⊙

Patrol officer: "Why did you drive into the ditch?"
Driver: "I was trying to turn off the blinker."

⊙⊙⊙

Sister Deena had just returned home from Sunday evening service when she was startled by a burglar. With great biblical authority she yelled, "Stop! Acts 2:38!" which implies "Turn from your sin."

The thief stopped dead in his tracks. Then the woman calmly called the police and explained what she had done.

As the officer cuffed the man, he asked the burglar, "Why did you stop your burgling? All the old lady did was yell a Bible verse at you."

"Bible verse?" replied the crook. "She said she had an ax and two .38s!"

Teacher: "Zach, you need to work on learning the presidents. When I was your age, I could name all of them."
Zach: "Yes, but then there were only four or five."

◉ ⊙ ◎

Homework Excuses:

"I left it in my shirt, and my mother put it into the washing machine."
"My sister used it to line the rabbit's cage."
"A sudden gust of wind blew it out of my hand, and I never saw it again."
"My friend fell into a lake, and I jumped in to rescue him. My homework didn't make it, though."
"Our furnace stopped working, and we had to burn it to keep ourselves from freezing."
"I didn't do it because I didn't want the other kids in the class to look bad."
"I know the importance of recycling, so I did my part by recycling it."
"I didn't do it because I didn't want to add to your already-heavy workload."
"I lost it fighting this kid who said you *weren't* the best teacher in the whole world."

◉ ⊙ ◎

How do librarians catch fish?
With bookworms.

Knock-knock.
Who's there?
Aileen.
Aileen who?
Aileen piece of meat is good for the waistline.

Knock-knock.
Who's there?
Theodore.
Theodore who?
Theodore got slammed on my nose.

Knock-knock.
Who's there?
Dewey.
Dewey who?
Dewey have to keep telling these dumb jokes?

Ed: "How's your job at the travel agency?"
Ned: "Terrible. I'm not going anywhere."

⊙⊙⊙

What do you call a bone specialist from Egypt?
A Cairopractor.

⊙⊙⊙

The manager of a glass and window company advertised in the paper for experienced glaziers. Since a good glass man is hard to find, he was pleased when a man who called about the job said he had twelve years of experience.

"Where have you worked as a glazier?" the manager asked.

The man replied, "Krispy Kreme."

It was local election time, and the candidate was visiting all the houses in his area. At one house, a small boy answered the door.

"Tell me, young man," said the politician, "is your Mommy in the Republican Party or the Democratic Party?"

"Neither," said the child. "She's in the bathroom."

◉◉◉

Definitions:

Monologue: A conversation between a politician and somebody else.

Diplomacy: The art of letting someone else have your own way.

Minority Rule: A newborn baby just home from the hospital.

◉◉◉

A politician asked a minister, "What is something the government can do to help the church?"

"Well," the minister replied, "quit making one-dollar bills."

Two American GIs in World War II were crouched in a foxhole as night fell. One closed his eyes and thanked the Lord out loud for bringing him through another day.

"You know," said his buddy, "a lot of Germans are Christians. They pray to God just like we do. I bet some of 'em are over there prayin' that same prayer right now."

The other GI thought that over a few minutes, then wondered aloud, "Do you really think the Lord understands German?"

☉☉☉

Army doctor: "You're looking pale, Corporal. When did you eat last?"
Corporal: "Nineteen fifty-nine, sir."
Army doctor: "What? How could you survive so long?"
Corporal: "Well, sir, it's only 2130 now."

☉☉☉

An African dictator was invited to inspect his air force's new amphibious aircraft. He piloted it himself, and everything went fine until he prepared to land at the airport.

"Excuse me, sir," said his nervous copilot, "but it would be better to land on the lake, since the plane has pontoons."

The dictator swung the plane out over the lake and made a fair landing. Rising from his seat, he thanked his nervous copilot for his tact in avoiding a horrible mistake, then opened the door and stepped straight into the lake.

There was a church where the preacher and the minister of music were not getting along. As time went by, this spirit began to spill over into the worship service.

The first week the preacher preached on commitment and how we should all dedicate ourselves to God. The music director led the song, "I Shall Not Be Moved."

The second week the preacher preached on tithing and how we all should gladly give to the work of the Lord. The director led the song, "Jesus Paid It All."

The third week the preacher preached on gossiping and how we should all watch our tongues. The music director led, "I Love to Tell the Story."

With all this going on, the preacher became totally disgusted over the situation and the following Sunday told the congregation that he was considering resigning. The music director led, "Oh, Why Not Tonight?"

As it came to pass, the preacher did resign. The next week he informed the church that it was Jesus who led him there and it was Jesus who was taking him away. The music leader led the song, "What a Friend We Have in Jesus."

◉ ◉ ◉

A minister preached a very short sermon. He explained, "My dog got into my study and chewed up some of my notes."

At the close of the service a visitor asked, "If your dog ever has pups, please let my pastor have one of them."

◉ ◉ ◉

A sign painter is quizzing a robed prophet of doom. He says, "You want that sign to read THE WORLD ENDS TOMORROW. . . . When do you have to have it?"

A man walked into the office of a psychiatrist and sat down to explain his problem: "Doctor, I have this problem," the man said. "I keep hallucinating that I'm a dog. It's crazy. I don't know what to do!"

"A common canine complex," said the doctor reassuringly. "Relax. Come here and lie down on the couch."

"Oh, I can't, doctor," the man said nervously. "I'm not allowed up on the furniture."

⊙⊙⊙

Fred: "Someone said that you look like an owl."
Meg: "Who?"
Fred: "You sound like one, too."

⊙⊙⊙

Who's a better boxer: a bean or a chicken?
The bean—he's no chicken.

The trouble with the world today is that when we give up that hour in April, no one feels sure we'll get it back in the fall.

⊙⊙⊙

Folks throughout the city knew they were in trouble when the new owners of the *Tribune* suavely altered the paper's time-honored motto to read: ALL THE NEWS THAT'S FIT FOR US.

⊙⊙⊙

A small town is where you can finish your Sunday paper at breakfast.

Joe: "That was the best inning I ever played."
Cricket captain: "Well, you mustn't let that discourage you."

The coach asked his assistant, "What's that new fullback's name?"

The assistant said, "He's from Thailand. His name is Bandanakadriyariki."

The coach said, "I hope he's good. That'll get me even with the newspapers."

Liz: "What has a hundred legs and lives on yogurt?"
Jen: "An aerobics class."

I can sizzle like bacon, and I am made with an egg.
I have plenty of backbone, but lack a good leg.
I peel layers like an onion, but still remain whole.
I can be long, like a flagpole; yet fit in a hole.
What am I?
A snake.

What kind of umbrella do most people carry on a rainy day?
A wet one.

Thousands hoard gold in this house, but no human built it. Spears are busy keeping watch, but no human guards it.
What is it?
A beehive.

"When Abraham Lincoln was your age," a man said to his lazy teenage son, "he was chopping wood, plowing, and hunting for food."

"When he was your age," the boy responded, "he was president of the United States."

⊙⊙⊙

Junior: "Mom, the new baby looks just like Rover."
Mom: "Junior, don't say such a thing."
Junior: "It's okay, Mom. Rover can't hear me."

⊙⊙⊙

A rich man and a poor man were arguing about which was happiest.

"My millions make me extremely happy," said the rich man. "Money assures me of excellent housing, fine cars, the best food, vacations whenever and wherever I want, the best possible medical treatment and total security. All you have to show are six children and a lot of debt."

"But I'm more contented than you," countered the poor man. "If I had your money, I'd want more. If you had six children, you wouldn't want any more."

What would you get if you crossed an airplane, an automobile, and a dog?
A flying car-pet.

⊙⊙⊚

After watching a news account of an airline crash, a teenager was asking his mother about the vital "black box" that's so important to accident investigators.

"It contains a complete record of the plane's diagnostics right up to the instant of the crash," she explained.

"Why isn't it destroyed on impact?"

"Because it's encased in a very special alloy material, I'm sure."

"Then why can't they make the whole airplane out of it?"

⊙⊙⊚

What kind of running means you will have to walk?
Running out of gas.

Patient: "Nurse, nurse!"
Nurse: "What is it, sir?"
Patient: "I keep seeing spots in front of my eyes."
Nurse: "Have you seen a doctor?"
Patient: "No, just spots."

◉⦿◎

How is a surgeon like a comedian?
They both keep you in stitches.

◉⦿◎

Hilda: What do fishermen and hypochondriacs have in common?"
Joe: "They don't really have to catch anything to be happy."

Knock-knock.
Who's there?
Dishes.
Dishes who?
Dishes the police. Open the door.

◉⊙◎

The Chancellor of England, Lord Bacon, about to sentence a criminal, asked if he had anything to say.

"Yes, Your Honor. You should let me off, because we're related. My name is Hogg, and Hogg is kin to Bacon."

"Not," Lord Bacon replied, "until it's hung."

◉⊙◎

Why was the butcher arrested?
The police caught him chop-lifting.

Why did the student take her math homework to gym class?
She wanted to work out her problems.

◉⊙◎

You Might Be a College Student If...

You have ever price-shopped for Top Ramen.
You have ever written a check for forty-five cents.
You celebrate when you find a quarter.
You have ever seen two consecutive sunrises without sleeping.
You can pack your worldly possessions into the back of a pickup (in one trip).
Your trash is overflowing and your bank account isn't.
You are personally keeping the local pizza place from bankruptcy.
You can sleep through your roommate's blaring stereo.
Your breakfast consists of a Coke on the way to class.
Your social life consists of a date with the library.
You live in an area that is smaller than most mobile homes.

◉⊙◎

Teacher: "I just don't understand how one person can make this many mistakes on her homework!"
Ellen: "It wasn't one person. My dad helped me."

Knock-knock.
Who's there?
Diesel.
Diesel who?
Diesel make you laugh.

⊙⊙⊙

Knock-knock.
Who's there?
Mandy.
Mandy who?
Mandy torpedoes—full speed ahead!

⊙⊙⊙

Knock-knock.
Who's there?
Little old lady.
Little old lady who?
Gee, I didn't know you could yodel!

Day
209

Mike: "What do you do for a living?"

Harvey: "I get fired every day."

Mike: "How can you earn a living by getting fired every day?"

Harvey: "I'm the star of the circus—the guy they call the Human Cannonball."

☉☉☉

Definitions:

Computer Programmer: A happy-go-lucky human trained to consume seven pizzas a week and interrupt normal conversations to consult aloud with imaginary colleagues.

Electrician: Someone who's always wiring for more money.

Historian: Someone who just can't let the past lie.

Mountain Climber: An athlete with the gift of grab.

Nuclear Scientist: A professional with a lot of ions in the fire.

Professional Golfer: A person who earns a living by playing a round.

Scorekeeper: The symphony orchestra's librarian.

Short-Order Cook: A person who prepares food for children.

Stagecoach: A theatrical instructor.

Violinist: A musician who does nothing but fiddle around.

☉☉☉

"What do you think of Shakespeare?" one student asked another.

The other shrugged. "All of his writing is really just a collection of well-known quotations thrown together into somewhat cohesive plots."

An American president once called a break from a long cabinet meeting and strolled onto the White House lawn to gather his thoughts. He placed a hand on a garden rail and stood staring across the grass. For five full minutes, the president didn't move a muscle.

"He's really torn by this one," one cabinet official said quietly to another. "I've never before seen him this deep in thought."

Another five minutes passed, and the nation's highest officials looked on nervously as the president continued to stand perfectly still.

Eventually, the chief executive motioned for his cabinet to gather around him at the rail.

"See that squirrel out there?" he asked, pointing. "It hasn't flinched for more than ten minutes. I do believe it's dead."

◉⊙◎

Where do polar bears vote?
The North Poll.

◉⊙◎

"Suppose you were an idiot, and suppose you were a member of Congress. . . . But I repeat myself." Will Rogers

"March Madness" also describes the mood of anyone working on income tax forms.

⊙⊙⊙

A man wrote a letter to the IRS: "I have been unable to sleep, knowing that I have cheated on my income tax. I understated my taxable income and have enclosed a check for two hundred dollars. If I still can't sleep, I will send the rest."

⊙⊙⊙

It's easy for anyone to meet expenses. You find them everywhere.

What was Moby Dick's favorite dinner?
Fish and ships.

⊙⊙⊙

Who loves to solve mysteries and soak in bubble baths?
Sherlock Foams.

⊙⊙⊙

Knock-knock.
Who's there?
Tom Sawyer.
Tom Sawyer who?
Tom Sawyer holey sock.

A teenager was telling her father all about her new boy-friend.

"He sounds very nice," said her father. "Does he have any money?"

"You men are all alike," she said. "He asked the same thing about you."

A man asked his wife, "What would you most like for your birthday?"

She said, "Oh, I'd love to be ten again."

He came up with a plan, and, on the morning of her birthday, he took her to a theme park. They rode every ride in the park together.

Lunchtime soon came, so into McDonald's they went, where she was given a Big Mac with french fries and a milkshake. After lunch, he took her to a movie theater to watch the latest movie for kids—complete with popcorn and soda.

At last she staggered home with her husband and collapsed into bed. Her husband leaned over and asked, "So, sweetheart, what was it like being ten again?"

She looked at him and said quietly, "Actually, I meant the dress size."

"Marriage is a wonderful institution, but who wants to live in an institution?" —Groucho Marx

Celebrity: "It is so good to be with you wonderful people here at Shady Rest Nursing Home. Does anyone here know who I am?"
Resident: "No, but don't worry. If you go down to the front desk, they'll tell you."

◉◉◉

A reporter interviewed a 103-year-old woman:
    "And what is the best thing about being 103?" the reporter asked.
    The woman simply replied, "No peer pressure."

◉◉◉

How can time be such a wonderful healer—but such a terrible beautician?

What is the favorite musical of chickens?
Fiddler on the Roost.

⊙⊙⊙

What composer is the favorite among dogs?
Poochini.

⊙⊙⊙

Music History According to Students:

Bach was the most famous composer in the world, and so was Handel.

Handel was half German, half Italian, and half English. He was very large.

Bach died from 1750 to the present.

Beethoven wrote music even though he was deaf. He was so deaf he wrote loud music. He took long walks in the forest even when everyone was calling for him.

Beethoven expired in 1827 and later died for this.

Why is it a good idea to have a frog on your baseball team?
They're good at catching pop flies.

◉⊙◎

Aussie Mountain-Bike Slang:

Death Cookies: Fist-sized rocks that knock your bike in every direction but the one in which you want to proceed.

First Blood: Credit to the first rider in a group who crashes and starts bleeding as a result.

Fred: (1) A person who spends a lot of money on his bike and clothing but still can't ride. "What a fred—too much Lycra and titanium and not enough skill." (2) Synonym for poser.

Gravity Check: A fall.

JRA: Acronym for "Just Riding Along," a phrase universally uttered by people bringing both halves of their frame and the remains of their fork in for warranty replacement.

Vultures: Spectators who line up at dangerous obstacles in hopes of seeing blood.

Weigh-In Weenie: An MTB owner who is more concerned with how many milligrams a certain component saves off the bike's total weight than with how to be a better rider.

◉⊙◎

If swimming is so good for your figure, how do you explain whales?

The beginning of eternity;
The end of time and space.
The beginning of every end,
And the end of every place.
What am I?
The letter E.

⊚⊙⊚

Why was the library so tall?
Because it had the most stories.

⊚⊙⊚

Maggie woke up one day with a toothache and went to the only dental practice in town to have it fixed. The dental practice had two partners, Dr. Smith and Dr. Jones. Dr. Smith has a beautiful smile, while Dr. Jones has a mouth of ugly, crooked teeth. Who should Maggie see about the toothache?

Dr. Jones. Since it is the only dental practice in town, Dr. Jones must fix Dr. Smith's teeth and vice versa.

Mandy came crying to her dad. Between sobs, she explained that she'd traded her pet kitten Jingles to the children at the refreshment stand down the street for a cold drink.

"I see," he said, knowingly. "And now you miss little Jingles, don't you?"

"No," she said, "but I'm still thirsty, and I don't have anything else to trade."

⊙⊙⊙

Fred: "I come from a musical family."
Peggy: "I never knew that."
Fred: "Oh yes, Dad drummed his fingers, Aunt Mae blew her nose, and Grandpa fiddled with his mustache."

⊙⊙⊙

After being punished for losing his temper, a little boy ventured to say to his mother, "Please explain to me the difference between my foul temper and your worn nerves."

A young man was boarding an airplane for his first flight. He was very bashful, and found to his dismay that he'd been assigned a center seat between two attractive young ladies.

Settling in with far more discomfort than normally attends airline travel in a center seat, he wondered what to say or how to act. The words of a dear old uncle happily came to him: "Whenever you're around women you don't know, just ask them if they're married and if they have any children, and they'll do all the talking after that."

He braced himself and turned to the woman on his left. "Do you have any children?"

"Why, yes!" she answered eagerly. "A gorgeous little girl named Heather."

"Are you married?" he continued.

Her friendliness instantly became ice, and she returned to the magazine she'd been reading.

"Must've asked the questions in the wrong order," he thought to himself.

He turned to the woman on his right. "Are you married?" he asked.

"Well. . .no," she responded suspiciously.

"Do you have any children?"

◉ ◉ ◉

Passenger: "Are you sure this train stops at San Francisco?"
Conductor: "If it doesn't, you'll hear an awful splash."

◉ ◉ ◉

Where do you find good sandwiches in India?
Try New Delhi.

Tom: "What is the first thing you lose on a diet?"
Dot: "Your patience."

⊙⊙⊙

Diet Rules:

If you eat something and no one sees you eat it, it has no
calories.
If you drink a diet soda with a candy bar, the calories in the
candy bar are canceled out by the diet soda.
When you eat with someone, the calories don't count if you
don't eat more than he or she does.
Foods such as hot chocolate, pancakes, and Sara Lee
cheesecake used for medicinal purposes never count.
If you fatten up everyone else around you, then you look
thinner.
Movie-related food, such as Milk Duds, buttered popcorn,
Junior Mints, Red Hots, and Tootsie Rolls are okay to
eat, because you do it in the dark.
Cookie pieces contain no calories. The process of breaking
causes calorie leakage.
Stuff licked off knives and spoons have no calories if you are
preparing something to eat.
Foods of the same color—like spinach and pistachio ice
cream—have the same number of calories.
Chocolate is a universal color and may be substituted for any
other food color.

⊙⊙⊙

What is the best diet for a golfer?
Greens only.

Why did Columbus sail to America?
It was faster than swimming.

◎◉◎

Geography Teacher: "Andrew, can you tell me where Amsterdam is?"
Andrew: "Er—here it is! Page 75!"

◎◉◎

Ancient History According to Students:

Without the Greeks, we wouldn't have history. The Greeks invented columns and myths. One myth says that the mother of Achilles dipped him in the River Stynx until he became intolerable. Achilles appears in *The Iliad*, by Homer. Homer also wrote *The Oddity*, in which Penelope was the last hardship that Ulysses endured on his journey. Actually, Homer was not written by Homer but by another man of that name.

Socrates was a famous Greek teacher who went around giving people advice. They killed him. Socrates died from an overdose of wedlock.

In the Olympic games, Greeks ran races, hurled the biscuits, and threw the java. The reward to the victor was a coral wreath.

There were no wars in Greece, as the mountains were so high that they couldn't climb over to see what their neighbors were doing.

When they fought with the Persians, the Greeks were outnumbered because the Persians had more men.

Eventually, the Romans conquered the Greeks.

At Roman banquets, the guests wore garlic in their hair.

Julius Caesar extinguished himself on the battlefields of Gaul.

Teacher: "How long did the Hundred Years' War last?"

Student: "I don't know. Ten years?"

Teacher: "No! Think carefully. How old is a five-year-old horse?"

Student, thoughtfully: "Oh, five years old!"

Teacher: "That's right. So how long did the Hundred Years' War last?"

Student: "Now I get it—five years!"

⊙⊙⊚

A linguistics professor was lecturing his class one day. "In the English language," he said, "a double negative forms a positive. In other languages, such as Russian, a double negative is still a negative. However, there is no language wherein a double positive can form a negative."

A voice from the back of the room said, "Yeah, right."

⊙⊙⊚

A rule was posted in large letters in the school hallway: SHOES REQUIRED IN THE CAFETERIA.

In the margin, someone had scribbled: SOCKS MUST GO TO THE GYM.

Knock-knock.
Who's there?
Hominy.
Hominy who?
Hominy doughnuts can you eat?

⊙⊙⊙

Knock-knock.
Who's there?
Honey hive.
Honey hive who?
Honey, hive got a crush on you.

⊙⊙⊙

Knock-knock.
Who's there?
Cashew.
Cashew who?
Cashew see I'm freezing out here?

**Day
224**

As Noah and his family were disembarking from the ark, they paused on a ridge to look back.

"We should have done something, Noah," his wife said. "That old hulk of an ark will sit there and be an eyesore on the landscape for years to come."

"Everything's taken care of," Noah assured her. "I left the two termites aboard."

◉◉◉

A good sermon is one that goes in one ear, out the other—and smacks somebody else right between the eyes.

◉◉◉

You Might Be a Missionary or Missionary's Kid If...

You don't think two hours is a long sermon.
You refer to gravel roads as highways.
Fitting fifteen or more people into a car seems normal.
You realize that furlough is not a vacation.
You do your devotions in another language.
You speak with authority on the subject of airline travel.
You can cut grass with a machete but can't start a lawnmower.
You watch nature documentaries and think how good that animal would taste if it were fried.
You can't answer the question, "Where are you from?"

Man: "Are you certain this dog you're selling me is loyal?"
Owner: "Of course he sure is. I've sold him five times, and
every time he's come back."

⊙⊙⊙

What kind of bird does construction work?
The crane.

⊙⊙⊙

A police officer saw a woman sitting in her car with a tiger
in the front seat next to her. The officer said, "It's against the
law to have that tiger in your car. Take him to the zoo."

The next day the police officer saw the same woman in the
same car with the same tiger. He said, "I told you yesterday to
take that tiger to the zoo!"

The woman replied, "I did. He had such a good time, today
we're going to the beach!"

"I fish, therefore I lie." Anonymous

◉◉◉

One NFL team has had so many members experience run-ins with the law, it's adopted a new honor system: "Yes, your Honor. No, your Honor."

When you see four of this team's players in a car, know who's driving? The police.

◉◉◉

There's a good reason some people can't seem to mind their own business. Usually, it's because they have either (1) no mind or (2) no business.

Jake: "Our town's baseball league is the worst!"

Jock: "How bad is it?"

Jake: "It's so bad the kids throw away the baseball cards and collect the bubble gum."

◉◉◉

Heckling umpires can be an art form. Three favorite put-downs are:

"Hey, ump, if you follow the white line, you'll find first base."

"Hey, ump, how can you sleep with all the lights on?"

"Hey, ump, shake your head—your eyes are stuck."

◉◉◉

Fran: "Why didn't the first baseman get to dance with Cinderella?"

Dan: "He missed the ball."

What never gets sick but is always broken out with twenty-one spots?
A six-sided die.

◉☉◉

Lovely and round,
I shine with pale light,
Grown in the darkness,
A lady's delight.
What am I?
A pearl.

◉☉◉

What dog can jump higher than a tree?
Any dog can jump higher than a tree. Trees don't jump.

A teenager asked his lifeguard friend, "What's the best way to teach a girl to swim?"

His buddy thought a moment. "Is she your sister or your girlfriend?"

"My sister."

"Well, I'd suggest the old-fashioned way. Push her into the pool and tell her she's got a choice: Sink or swim."

⊙⊙⊙

A family was at the zoo, watching an elephant snarf up peanuts with its trunk.

"Daddy," the small daughter asked, "is that long thing in front a vacuum cleaner?"

⊙⊙⊙

Hotel guest: "Hello, room service. Send up two burned eggs, undercooked bacon, cold toast, and weak coffee."

Room service: "Why do you want such a terrible breakfast?"

Hotel guest: "I'm homesick."

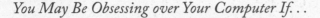

You May Be Obsessing over Your Computer If. . .

You turn off your computer and get an awful empty feeling, as if you just pulled the plug on a loved one.

You start using smileys :-) in your snail mail.

You find yourself typing "com" after every period when using a word processor.com

You can't correspond with your mother, since she doesn't have a computer.

In real-life conversations, you don't laugh, you just say, "LOL, LOL."

You move into a new house and you decide to "Netscape" before you landscape.

When your inbox shows "no new messages," you feel really depressed

You wake up at four o'clock in the morning to go to the bathroom and stop to check your e-mail on the way back to bed.

◉⊙◎

Has anyone noticed that it now costs more to entertain the average teenager than it cost to put both of the youth's parents through college?

◉⊙◎

Doctor: "I'm afraid you have a dangerously advanced case of bronchitis."

Patient: "I only had the sniffles when I first sat down in your waiting room."

A certain bathroom-scale manufacturer was very proud of the new model being introduced at the trade fair: "It's calibrated to one one-hundredth of a pound; it can measure your height in feet or meters; it gives you a readout via an LED or human voice simulator; and that's not all. . . ."

"Very impressive," interrupted a not-too-slender home-furnishings sales rep, "but before I place an order I'll have to try it out."

No sooner had the sales rep stepped on the scale than a loud, very human-sounding voice issued forth: "One at a time, please, one at a time."

◉⊙◉

The old family physician took his son into partnership after the young man received his medical degree. The old doctor then went off on a two-week vacation, his first in years.

When he got home, he asked his son if there'd been any problems at the clinic. The son said no, everything went well. "In fact," he said, "you know that rich old widow, Mrs. Ferguson? I cured her of her chronic indigestion."

"Well, that's fine," said the old doctor. "But Mrs. Ferguson's indigestion is what put you through medical school."

◉⊙◉

Knock-knock.
Who's there?
Crummy.
Crummy who?
How the cookie felt when he went to the doctor.

What do math teachers like to eat with their coffee?
A slice of pi.

⊙⊙⊙

Did you hear about the new restaurant that just opened on the moon? Good food, but no atmosphere.

⊙⊙⊙

The Top Five Signs You're a Lousy Cook:

5. Your family automatically heads for the table every time they hear the smoke alarm.
4. Your kids know what "peas porridge in the pot nine days old" tastes like.
3. Your kids' favorite smoothie is Pepto-Bismol.
2. No matter what you do, the gravy still turns bright purple.
1. You burned the house down trying to make freezer jam.

Why is a moon rock tastier than an earth rock?
Because it's a little meteor.

⊙⊙⊙

One astronaut asks another astronaut if he has ever heard of the planet Saturn.

The second astronaut says, "I'm not sure, but it has a familiar ring."

⊙⊙⊙

An astronaut graduated near the bottom of his class. On his first mission into space, he was teamed with an orangutan. The astronaut and the orangutan were each given an envelope that they were to open once they were in space.

Moments after blastoff, the orangutan opened his envelope, read the contents, and then began flicking buttons and hitting switches.

Eagerly opening his envelope, the astronaut was surprised to discover three words of instruction: "Feed the orangutan."

Lady: "My husband bumped his head at work, and now he thinks he's a giant pecan."
Lawyer: "Oh, no! Another nut case."

◉⊙◎

What's a good name for a lawyer?
Sue.

◉⊙◎

Judge: "Have you ever held up a train?"
Outlaw: "Now and then."
Judge: "Where have you held up trains?"
Outlaw: "Here and there."
Judge: "What things have you taken from passengers?"
Outlaw: "This and that."
Judge: "Sheriff, lock this man up!"
Outlaw: "Hey! When do I get out of jail?"
Judge: "Oh, sooner or later."

Teacher: "Do you think it was just as easy to explore the Arctic as it was to explore Antarctica?"

Student: "I don't know. . . . There's a world of difference."

⊙⊙⊚

Answers to Fifth-Grade Science Exams:

H_2O is hot water, and CO_2 is cold water.

Nitrogen is not found in Ireland because it is not found in a free state.

To collect fumes of sulfur, hold a deacon over a flame in a test tube.

A fossil is an extinct animal. The older it is, the more extinct it is.

When you smell an odorless gas, it is probably carbon monoxide.

Three kinds of blood vessels are arteries, vanes, and caterpillars.

Dew is formed on leaves when the sun shines down on them and makes them perspire.

Mushrooms always grow in damp places and so they look like umbrellas.

The pistol of a flower is its only protection against insects.

Respiration is composed of two acts: first inspiration and then expectoration.

When you breathe, you inspire. When you do not breathe, you expire.

⊙⊙⊚

What happened to the principal who fell into the copying machine?

She was beside herself!

Knock-knock.
Who's there?
Grover.
Grover who?
Grover there and get me a cookie.

◉ ◉ ◉

Knock-knock.
Who's there?
Tank.
Tank who?
You're welcome.

◉ ◉ ◉

Knock-knock.
Who's there?
Hummus.
Hummus who?
"Hummus remember this, a kiss is just a kiss."

Day
237

The Sunday school teacher, trying to get a response from his class of eight-year-old boys, said, "Boys, can't you imagine Noah, on that ark, spending a lot of time fishing?"

One boy replied, "I don't think he did. He had only two worms!"

⊙⊙⊙

The simplest and best decisions are those that did not have to find their way through committees or channels. Consider, for example, the Ten Commandments.

⊙⊙⊙

Bert and Ernie are two Christians who have lived very good and healthy lives. They die and arrive in heaven. Walking along one of the golden streets and marveling at all the paradise around them, Ernie turns to Bert and says, "Wow. I never knew heaven was going to be as good as this."

"Yeah," says Bert. "And just think, if we hadn't eaten all that oat bran, we could have gotten here ten years earlier."

Why was the rabbit so unhappy?
She was having a bad hare day.

◉◉◉

A man took his rottweiler to the vet and said to him, "My dog is cross-eyed. Is there anything you can do for him?"

"Well," said the vet, "let me take a look at him." So he picked up the dog and had a good look at his eyes.

"Well," said the vet, "I'm going to have to put him down."

"Just because he's cross-eyed?" asked the man.

"No," said the vet, "because he's heavy."

◉◉◉

What did one horse say to the other horse?
The pace is familiar, but I can't remember the mane.

Why won't banks allow kangaroos to open accounts?
Their checks always bounce.

⊙⊙⊚

A kid swallowed a coin and it got stuck in his throat. His mother yelled for help. A man passing by hit him in the small of the back, and the coin popped out.

"I don't know how to thank you, Doctor. . . ," the boy's mother started.

"I'm not a doctor, ma'am," the man explained. "I'm from the IRS."

⊙⊙⊚

What is the favorite mode of transportation for accountants?
Tax-is.

Announcement at a Fourth of July Celebration: "Senator Jones will now make a speech. Immediately afterward, we will have an egg-throwing contest."

◉ ⊙ ◎

Father: "You never know what you can do until you try."
Son: "I guess you never know what you *can't* do until you try, either."

◉ ⊙ ◎

It's always better to say nothing and have people wonder about your intelligence than to say something stupid and leave them no doubt.

It was only her second date with a diehard baseball fan, and Judy was a little nervous. It was her fault they arrived at the ballpark a full hour after the game had started.

Taking her seat, Judy glanced up at the scoreboard. It was a tight pitcher's battle, bottom of the fifth, 0–0. "Look, Charlie," she exclaimed with relief, "we haven't missed a thing!"

◉◉◉

Mike: "Why did the chicken cross the basketball court?"
Ike: "Because it heard the referee calling fouls."

◉◉◉

The captain of a team says to the ref, "My coach wants to know if there is a penalty for thinking."

The ref says, "No."

The captain says, "Well, my coach thinks you're blind!"

What do you call something that everyone asks for, everyone gives, everyone needs, but very few people take?
Advice.

⊙⊙⊙

What do you get from a pampered cow?
Spoiled milk.

⊙⊙⊙

Linda was making peach jam. She put all the peaches in the pot and began to cook them. Then she remembered she had to add one cup of sugar for every two peaches. How did she figure out how much sugar to put?
She counted the pits.

There's no such thing as a beautiful newborn baby—until you become a parent.

◉◉◉

Mother: "Troy, I've been calling you for the last five minutes! Didn't you hear me?"

Troy: "No, I didn't hear you until the fourth time you called."

◉◉◉

It's a sunny morning in the big forest, and the Bear family is just waking up.

Baby Bear goes downstairs and sits in his small chair at the table. He looks into his small bowl. It's empty! "Who's been eating my porridge?" he squeaks.

Daddy Bear comes to the table and sits in his big chair. He looks into his big bowl. It's also empty! "Who's been eating my porridge?" he roars.

Mommy Bear calls from the kitchen, "How many times do we have to go through this? It was Mommy Bear who got up first. It was Mommy Bear who woke everybody up. It was Mommy Bear who unloaded the dishwasher. It was Mommy Bear who went out to get the newspaper. It was Mommy Bear who set the table. It was Mommy Bear who put the cat out, cleaned the litter box, and filled the cat's water and food dish. And now that you've finally decided to come downstairs and start your day, listen well because I'm only going to say this one time—I haven't had time to make the porridge yet!"

What was the snail doing on the highway?
About one mile a day.

⊙⊙⊙

Donald: "I hear you broke off your engagement. What happened?"
Daisy: "Oh, it's just that my feelings for him have changed."
Donald: "Are you returning the ring?"
Daisy: "Oh, no. My feelings for the ring haven't changed."

⊙⊙⊙

What Men Really Mean:

"Take a break, honey, you're working too hard" really means: "I can't hear the game over the vacuum cleaner."

"Can I help you with dinner?" really means: "Why isn't it on the table yet?"

"I missed you" really means: "My socks need washing, and we're out of toilet paper."

"You look terrific!" really means: "Please don't try anything else on; I'm starved."

"I can't find it" really means: "It didn't fall into my outstretched hands."

"She's one of those rabid feminists" really means: "She won't wait on me hand and foot."

"Honey, we don't need material things to prove our love" really means: "I forgot our anniversary again."

"That's interesting, dear" really means: "Are you still talking?"

Day 245

Al: "You sure seem unhappy."

Hal: "Yep. Living with my mother-in-law is really stressful. She's constantly fussing at both me and my wife."

Al: "Well, if worse comes to worst, you may have to ask her to move out."

Hal: "I don't think we can do that. It's her house."

◉⊙◎

Some teenaged friends were marveling at the scene of an accident where one of them miraculously had walked away from the mishap without a scratch the night before.

"Wow, that was some smashup," said one.

"Totaled the car," said another.

"How'd it happen?" asked a third.

The victim pointed to a tilted telephone pole. "See that?"

"Yeah."

"I didn't."

◉⊙◎

What is yellow and arrives at the door to make a mother's load lighter?

The school bus.

Mr. Johnson was overweight, so his doctor put him on a diet. He said, "I want you to eat regularly for two days, then skip a day, and repeat this procedure for two weeks. The next time I see you, you should have lost at least five pounds."

When Mr. Johnson returned, he shocked the doctor by having dropped almost twenty-five pounds.

"That's incredible!" the doctor told him. "You did this just by following my instructions?"

The slimmed-down Mr. Johnson nodded. "I'll tell you, though, I thought I was going to drop dead that third day."

"From hunger, you mean?"

"No," replied Mr. Johnson, "from skipping."

◉⊙◉

A hefty gentleman stepped onto a pay scale and put in a dime. He was not amused when the machine registered this message: ONE CUSTOMER PER DIME.

◉⊙◉

A couple was enjoying a dinner party at the home of friends. Near the end of the meal, the wife slapped her husband's arm.

"That's the third time you've gone for dessert," she said. "The hostess must think you're an absolute pig."

"I doubt that," the husband said. "I've been telling her it's for you."

How did they catch the crooks at the pig farm?
Someone squealed.

⊙⊙⊙

In a small town the veterinarian, who was also the chief of police, was awakened by the telephone.

"Please hurry!" said the woman's voice on the other end of the line.

"Do you need the police or a vet?" he asked.

"Both," the woman replied. "I'm not able to get my dog's mouth open, and there's a burglar's leg in it."

⊙⊙⊙

A cop pulls a woman over and says, "Let me see your driver's license, lady."

The woman replies, "I wish you people would get your act together. One day you take away my license and the next day you ask me to show it."

A college student delivered a pizza to the Wilsons' house. Mr. Wilson asked him, "What is the usual tip?"

"Well," he replied, "this is my first trip here, but the other guys say if I get a quarter out of you, I'll be doing great."

"Is that so?" snorted Mr. Wilson. "Well, just to show them how wrong they are, I'll give you five dollars."

"Thanks!" replied the delivery guy. "I'll put this toward my textbooks."

"What are you studying?" asked Mr. Wilson.

The young man smiled and said, "Psychology."

◉⊙◎

A college student remembered his father's birthday was just days away. He sent a cheap present with a note reading, "Dear Dad, I know this isn't much, but it's all you can afford."

◉⊙◎

Teacher: "Mrs. Baker, I've called you today to discuss Brooke's appearance."

Mrs. Baker: "Why? What is wrong with her appearance?"

Teacher: "She hasn't made one in my classroom since September!"

Knock-knock.
Who's there?
Turnip.
Turnip who?
Turnip the stereo—I can't hear it.

⊙⊙⊙

Knock-knock
Who's there?
Venue.
Venue who?
"Venue vish upon a star."

⊙⊙⊙

Knock-knock.
Who's there?
Cereal.
Cereal who?
Cereal pleasure to meet you.

Day 250

A minister on vacation was reading his hometown newspaper. He was stunned to come across his own obituary. Shocked and not a little upset, he immediately telephoned the editor.

"I'm calling you long distance about the report of my death in your paper yesterday," he explained with great indignation.

"Yes, sir," came the calm reply. "And from where are you calling?"

⊙⊙⊙

Knock-knock.
Who's there?
Zeke.
Zeke who?
"Zeke and ye shall find."

⊙⊙⊙

Brenda: "How did Adam and Eve feel when expelled from the Garden of Eden?"
Sandy: "They were really put out."

What has four legs and flies?
A horse in the summertime.

◉◉◎

What is a pig's favorite play?
Hamlet.

◉◉◎

A snail starts a slow climb up the trunk of an apple tree. A sparrow observing his progress can't help laughing and says, "Don't you know there aren't any apples on the tree yet?"

"Yes," said the snail, "but there will be by the time I get up there."

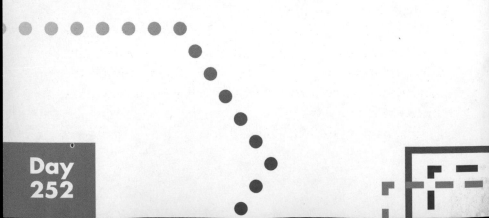

Josh: "My dad manages a whole chain of convenience stores."

Mia: "What does a manager do?"

Josh: "Goes around and trains the staff, counts the money, checks the locks to see that everything is secure. Since they're all open twenty-four hours a day, every day of the year, that's a big responsibility."

Mia: "If they're open round the clock. . .why do they have locks?"

⊙⊙⊙

Responses to the question "How's your job at the riding academy?"

"I'm saddled with a lot of work."

"I never have a free run."

"People ride me at work."

"The bucks aren't that good."

"I never get to horse around."

⊙⊙⊙

A young businessman had just started his own firm. He rented a beautiful office and had it furnished with the very best. Sitting at his fancy desk, he saw a man come into the outer office.

Wishing to appear busy to his potential first customer, he picked up the telephone and improvised a one-sided conversation with a big spender. He threw big figures around and made giant commitments. Finally he hung up and asked the visitor, "May I help you?"

The man answered, "Sure. I've come to install that phone!"

Day 253

Why did it take the weatherman so long to get dressed for work?
He couldn't find his wind socks.

⊙⊙⊙

A father was teaching his son to admire the beauty in nature.

"Look, Will," he exclaimed, "isn't that a beautiful sunset that God painted?"

"It sure is, Dad," the son agreed, "especially since God had to paint it with His left hand."

The father was bewildered. "What do you mean—His left hand?"

"Well," he said, "my Sunday school teacher said that Jesus is sitting on God's right hand."

⊙⊙⊙

What did the sun say when it was introduced to the earth?
"Pleased to heat you."

The wife of a U.S. Representative shook him awake one night.

"Jim, there's a robber in the house," she whispered. "Get up."

The representative mumbled in reply, "No, dear. In the Senate, yes. But not in the House."

◉◉◉

The campaigning Democrat was interrupted time after time by a man in the back of the crowd who kept proclaiming loudly that he was a Republican.

"And why are you a Republican?" the politician finally asked.

"My father was a Republican and his father before him!" the man yelled.

"Well, suppose your father and grandfather were fools. What would that make you?"

"A Democrat!"

◉◉◉

Citizen: "I've heard a great deal about you."
Politician: "Possibly. But you can't prove any of it."

What kind of animal cleans the ocean?
A mermaid!

⊙⊙⊙

Knock-knock.
Who's there?
Deluxe.
Deluxe who?
Deluxe Ness Monster.

⊙⊙⊙

How did Rapunzel find her missing hairbrush?
She combed the land.

Day 256

One cold winter day, a boy was standing outside a shoe store, praying to God for some socks or some shoes. Just then a lady walked up to him and said, "Is there something that I can help you with?"

He looked down at his feet and said, "Well, I would like some shoes."

She grabbed his hand and took him into the shoe store. She asked for a dozen pairs of socks and a pair of shoes. They sat down, and the clerk put a pair of socks and shoes on the boy.

As the woman got up to leave, the boy thanked her. She told him that if he ever needed anything else, to not to be afraid to ask.

He looked at her and asked, "Are you God's wife?"

◉ ◉ ◉

How do you catch a unique rabbit?
Unique up on it.

◉ ◉ ◉

How do you catch a tame rabbit?
Tame way. Unique up on it!

In the 1980 Olympics, the U.S. basketball team, coached by Bobby Knight, easily beat the Chinese team. When asked about the win, Bobby said, "It was a lot of fun playing the Chinese, but an hour later, we wanted to play them again!"

⊙⊙⊙

The late Joe E. Lewis used to say about golf, "I play in the low eighties. If it's any hotter than that, I won't play."

⊙⊙⊙

There are lots of small towns in the United States. One of them is Ferguson, Ohio. When you enter the city limits there is a sign that reads, WELCOME TO FERGUSON. BEWARE OF THE DOG. AND THE ALL-NIGHT DRUGSTORE CLOSES AT NOON.

"I play in the over-forty basketball league. We don't have jump balls. The ref just puts the ball on the floor, and whoever can bend over and pick it up gets possession."

◉⊙◎

If a boxer was knocked out by Dracula, what would he be?
He'd be out for the count.

◉⊙◎

P.E. Class Excuses:

"My son Peter is under doctor's care and should not take P. E. today. Please execute him."

"Please excuse Melody from class yesterday. She was sick and I had her shot."

"Dear Coach: Please excuse John from suiting-up on January 28, 29, 30, 31, 32, and also 33."

"Please excuse Roland from P. E. for a few days. Yesterday he fell out of a tree and misplaced his hip."

"John has not been in class because he had two teeth taken out of his face."

I am used to bat with, yet I never get a hit. I am near a ball,
yet it is never thrown.
What am I?
Eyelashes.

What do you call four Spaniards in quicksand?
Cuatro sinko.

I can be cool, but I am never cold.
I can be sorry, but I won't be guilty.
I can be spooked, but I can't be anxious.
I can be sweet, but I don't include candy.
I can be swallowed, but I will never be eaten.
What am I?
Words with double letters.

A nearsighted minister glanced at the note that Mrs. Edwards had sent to him by an usher.

The note read: "Phil Edwards having gone to sea, his wife desires the prayers of the congregation for his safety."

The minister failed to observe the punctuation, however, and surprised the congregation when he read aloud, "Phil Edwards, having gone to sea his wife, desires the prayers of the congregation for his safety."

◉⊙◎

What carries a weight in its belly, trees on its back, nails in its ribs, but has no feet?
A ship.

◉⊙◎

A band of pirates buried their treasure on the seashore. Afterward, the pirates looked around for a marker but could find nothing except a few ostrich eggs. So they broke open the eggs, fried the yolks, and left the shells on top of the buried treasure.

The pirate captain announced to his crew, "Eggs mark the spot."

Day
261

Knock-knock.
Who's there?
Pickle.
Pickle who?
Oh, that's my favorite musical instrument.

⊙⊙⊙

What is a pig's favorite ballet?
Swine Lake.

⊙⊙⊙

What fisherman's employment and Spanish instrument's name are the same?
Castanet.

Day 262

"I hear you have your brother's children spending the week with you," Darlene said to her friend Marla. "Counting your two, that makes five kids in one house. Wow! How are you feeling?"

"Outnumbered."

⊚⊙⊚

Teenager: "Dad, I got a very small scratch on the fender of your new car."
Father: "Oh no! Well, let me see. Where is it?"
Teenager: "In the trunk."

⊚⊙⊚

Two parents were sorting out the details of a fight between their children. After a few moments of chaos, as both youths simultaneously shouted versions of what had occurred, the parents called for quiet and asked them to report in turn.

"It all started," explained Dennis, trying to sound calm, "when Jeremy hit me back."

A couple vacationing in the Caribbean was irritated at the expected gratuities everywhere they turned. It seemed the pair couldn't enter a shop without some staff member opening the door, holding up a palm, and coughing meaningfully.

But the husband and wife's disaffection with the island changed. One afternoon as they swam in the surf, the husband was caught in an undertow and pulled out to sea. Cramps set in; he floundered and screamed. A lifeguard down the beach heard the cries, plunged in, took the man chin-in-elbow, hauled him to the beach, and successfully pumped his lungs clear.

The wife rushed to their villa and returned with her purse. "What's the going rate for this kind of thing?"

◉⊙◉

A con artist was trying to finesse a free train ride. When the conductor came down the aisle, the man pointed to his dog with a gesture of helpless agitation. "He ate my ticket!"

The conductor frowned. "Then I strongly suggest you buy him dessert."

◉⊙◉

A woman stepped up to a travel desk and asked for a round-trip ticket.

"Where to?" asked the agent.

The woman looked offended. "Right back here. Where do you think?"

"The X-ray shows a small spot under your kneecap, but it's probably just scar tissue," the doctor told the college quarterback. "I'm not very concerned about it."

The quarterback was not assured. "If it was your knee," he retorted, "I wouldn't be very concerned, either."

◉ ⊙ ◎

A Limerick

A dentist named Archibald Moss
Fell in love with the dainty Miss Ross.
But he held in abhorrence
Her Christian name, Florence,
So he renamed her his Dental Floss.

◉ ⊙ ◎

Doctor: "How is the boy who swallowed the quarter?"
Nurse: "No change yet."

Why do submarine captains have the best dental hygiene?
They use their Scope several times a day.

⊙⊙⊚

Through the pitch-black night, the captain sees a light dead ahead on a collision course with his ship. He sends a signal: "Change your course ten degrees east."

The light signals back: "Change yours ten degrees west."

Angry, the captain sends another signal: "I'm a navy captain! Change your course, sir!"

"I'm a seaman, second class," comes the reply. "Change your course, sir."

Now the captain is furious. "I'm a battleship! I'm not changing course!"

There is one last reply: "I'm a lighthouse. It's your call."

⊙⊙⊚

How does the navy get supplies to the sailors?
It ships them.

I am the briefest complete sentence in the English language. What am I?
I am! (Complete sentences always require a noun and verb. Imperative commands do not count.)

An English professor wrote the following words on the blackboard: "Woman without her man is nothing." He then requested that his students punctuate it correctly.

The men wrote: "Woman, without her man, is nothing."

The women wrote: "Woman! Without her, man is nothing."

A college junior was proudly showing off his new apartment to his friends. He led them into the living room.

"What are the big brass gong and hammer for?" one of his friends asked.

"That is my talking clock," he replied.

"How does it work?" his friend asked.

"I'll show you," the student said and proceeded to smash the gong with the hammer.

Suddenly, from the other side of the wall, a voice yelled, "Knock it off! It's 1:00 a.m.!"

Knock-knock.
Who's there?
Dime.
Dime who?
Dime to tell another one of these knock-knock jokes!

⊙⊙◎

Knock-knock.
Who's there?
Clark Kent.
Clark Kent who?
Clark Kent come—he's sick.

⊙⊙◎

Knock-knock.
Who's there?
Arnold.
Arnold who?
Arnold friend you haven't seen for years.

Worshipers were invited to a special study on prayer. At the close of the course, the pastor invited the participants to write one-sentence prayers. Here are some of those prayers:

"Lord, help me to relax about insignificant details—beginning at 7:41:23 a.m. (EST)."

"God, help me to consider people's feelings, even if most of them are hypersensitive."

"Father, help me take responsibility for my own actions, even though they're usually not my fault."

"Lord, help me to be more laid back, and help me do it exactly right."

"Heavenly Father, please help me take things more seriously, especially having a good time."

"God, give me patience, and I mean right now!"

"Lord, help me not to be a perfectionist. (Did I spell that correctly?)"

"Lord, keep me open to other people's ideas, wrong though they may be."

Amen.

◉⊙◉

Who was most sorry when the Prodigal Son returned home?
The fatted calf.

◉⊙◉

Teacher: "Georgie, why did you write in your essay that you're Jewish? I happen to know that your father is a minister."
Georgie: "I can't spell *Presbyterian!*"

What do you call a one-hundred-year-old ant?
An antique.

◉⊙◎

The manager of a large city zoo was composing a letter to order a pair of animals. He sat at his computer and typed, "I would like to order two mongooses, to be delivered at your earliest convenience."

He stared at the screen, focusing on the odd-looking word *mongooses*. Then he deleted the word and added another, so that the sentence now read: "I would like to place an order for two mongeese, to be delivered at your earliest convenience."

Once more he stared at the screen, this time analyzing the new word, which seemed just as strange as the original one. Finally, he deleted the whole sentence and started all over.

"Everyone knows no zoo should be without a mongoose," he typed. "Please send us two of them."

◉⊙◎

Why do birds fly south for the winter?
Because it's too far to walk.

The minister of Grace Church phoned the city's newspaper. "Thank you very much," he said, "for the error you made when you printed my sermon title on the church page. The topic I sent you was 'What Jesus Saw in a Publican.' You printed it as 'What Jesus Saw in a Republican.' I had the largest crowd of the year."

◉⊙◉

A lot of government policies make about as much sense as interstate highways in Hawaii.

◉⊙◉

After successfully getting their big line items approved in the congressional spending package, two lobbyists were celebrating at a Washington restaurant.

"You know," mused one, "it's a crying shame our grandchildren and great-grandchildren haven't been born yet so they can see the terrific things the government's doing with their money."

It's said that Albert Einstein was visited regularly in the afternoons by the eight-year-old daughter of a neighboring family. The mother apologized, but Einstein assured her it was a mutually beneficial friendship: He liked the jelly beans the girl brought him, and the youngster liked the way Einstein helped her with arithmetic.

⊙⊙⊙

Son: "Dad, what's middle age?"
Father: "That's when you lose all your growth at the top and do all your growing in the middle."

⊙⊙⊙

A successful novelist, being interviewed on a television talk show, lamented of burnout and self-doubt: "After twelve books and seven to eight million dollars in royalties, I finally realize I haven't the slightest talent for writing. Every one of my plots is just a rehash of things I've read by other writers."

"Are you telling us," hazarded the host, "that you're retiring?"

"Oh, of course not! Imagine what that would do to my reputation!"

What can be driven without any wheels and can be sliced without a knife?
A golf ball.

⊙⊙⊙

Football is not a contact sport. It's a collision sport. Dancing is a good example of a contact sport.

⊙⊙⊙

The pro football team had just finished its daily practice when a large turkey came strutting onto the field. While the players gazed in amazement, the turkey walked up to the head coach and demanded a tryout. Everyone stared in silence as the turkey caught pass after pass and ran through the defensive line.

When the turkey returned to the sidelines, the coach shouted, "You're terrific! Sign up for the season, and I'll see to it that you get a huge signing bonus."

"Forget the bonus," the turkey said. "All I want to know is, does the season go past Thanksgiving Day?"

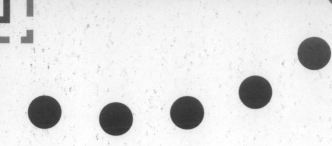

What question can you never answer with a "yes"?
"Are you sleeping?"

⊙⊙⊙

How do you name three consecutive days without using the words Monday, Tuesday, Wednesday, Thursday, Friday, Saturday, or Sunday?
Yesterday, Today, and Tomorrow!

⊙⊙⊙

What rock group has four members, all of whom are dead, one of whom was assassinated?
Mount Rushmore.

A teacher had just discussed magnets with her class. A bit later, she said, "My name begins with *M*, and I pick things up. What am I?"

Niles thought for a moment and answered, "Mom!"

◉◉◉

A frustrated father vented, "When I was a teenager and got in trouble, I was sent to my room without supper. But my son has his own television, telephone, computer, and CD player in his room."

"So what do you do to him?" asked his friend.

"I send him to *my* room!" exclaimed the father.

◉◉◉

A girl ran downstairs into the living room just as her parents were commenting on who her little brother looked like.

"I think he has your eyes," Mother was saying.

"And your nose," Father was adding.

"And now he's got Grandma's teeth!" the daughter interrupted.

What is a cat's favorite kind of computer?
A laptop.

◉◉◉

How do you know when a computer illiterate's been using your laptop?
There are eraser marks on the screen.

◉◉◉

Computer Quips:

"I haven't lost my mind—it's backed up on a disk somewhere."
"Spell-checkers are hear two stay."

Joined a health club last year—spent four hundred dollars. Haven't lost a pound. Apparently you gotta show up.

◉◉◉

The Top Ten Reasons We Are Overweight:

10. Hey, we get eighty channels of great television twenty-four hours a day. There's no time to exercise.
9. Girl Scout Cookies get better every year.
8. The colossal failure of the Salad King drive-thru franchise.
7. Just to spite Richard Simmons.
6. Addition of a diet soda does NOT mean your bacon cheeseburger/chili fries combo is a healthy meal.
5. We are still unconvinced that it's not really butter.
4. Fashion models are not good examples of real American women for our little girls.
3. Slim Fast tastes better with a scoop of Ben & Jerry's.
2. One word: Sprinkles!

And the number-one reason why we are overweight:

1. Did somebody say McDonald's?

◉◉◉

Harry: "Why do you eat so fast?"
Larry: "I want to eat as much as possible before I lose my appetite."

Day 277

What's a history teacher's favorite quiz show?
The Dating Game.

◎◉◎

Teacher: "Why are you reading the last pages of your history book first?"
Student: "I want to know how it ends."

◎◉◎

A history teacher was giving a verbal quiz. The focus was on the year 1912.

"What famous disaster occurred that year?" she asked.

Martin, the brash whiz kid of the class, predictably beat everyone to the answer. "The Titanic struck an iceberg!"

"Yes," said the teacher. "And where did it occur?"

"North Atlantic!" It was Martin again.

"What month?" pressed the teacher.

"April!" Martin piped up. "Twelfth of April!"

The teacher was becoming impatient with Martin's quick answers at the expense of everyone else.

"How many passengers and crew perished?" she pressed.

"One thousand five hundred seventeen!"

Martin was beaming, indomitable—until she turned squarely to face him with her last question: "And their names?"

A mother and father were paying bills one evening.

"Groceries, gasoline, electricity—everything is going up," mused the father.

"I know," agreed the mother. "Nothing ever goes down."

"Well, look at this!" exclaimed their son, walking into the room with his report card.

⊙⊙⊙

Teacher: "Class, are you looking forward to our field trip to the national tree museum?"

Student: "Well, I could take it or leaf it."

⊙⊙⊙

A man was visiting a college. He paused to admire the new Hemingway Hall that had recently been constructed on campus.

"It's marvelous to see a building named for Ernest Hemingway," he said.

"Actually," said the guide, "it's named for William Hemingway. No relation."

The visitor was astonished. "Was William Hemingway a writer, too?" he asked.

"Oh, yes," said his guide. "He wrote the check."

Knock-knock.
Who's there?
Warrior.
Warrior who?
Warrior been? I've been knocking for hours!

⊙⊙⊙

Knock-knock.
Who's there?
Boo!
Boo, who?
Well, you don't have to cry about it!

⊙⊙⊙

Knock-knock.
Who's there?
Anna.
Anna who?
Anna one, Anna two. . .

Day 280

What's worse than looking into the eye of a great white shark?
Looking into his tonsils.

◉⊙◎

The poor country parson was livid when he confronted his wife with the receipt for a 250 dollar dress she had bought. "How could you do this?" he exclaimed.

"I don't know," she wailed. "I was standing in the store looking at the dress. Then I found myself trying it on. It was like the devil was whispering to me, 'Wow, you look great in that dress. You should buy it.'"

"Well," the husband persisted, "you know how to deal with the tempter. Just tell him, 'Get behind me, Satan!'"

"I did," replied his wife, "but then he said, 'It looks great from back there, too!'"

◉⊙◎

A parsonage son said to his mother, "I've decided that I want to be a preacher so that I can clean up the mess the world is in."

"That's just wonderful," purred his mother. "You can go upstairs and start with your room."

To make it possible for everyone to attend church next Sunday, we are going to have a special "No-Excuse Sunday":

Cots will be placed in the foyer for those who say, "Sunday is my only day to sleep in."

There will be a special section with lounge chairs for those who feel that our pews are too hard.

We will have steel helmets for those who say, "The roof would cave in if I ever came to church."

Relatives and friends will be in attendance for those who can't go to church and cook dinner, too.

Doctors and nurses will be in attendance for those who plan to be sick on Sunday.

The sanctuary will be decorated with both Christmas poinsettias and Easter lilies for those who have never seen the church without them.

◉☉◎

Did you hear the story about the peacock that crossed the road? It is really a colorful tail. . . .

◉☉◎

"No wonder nobody comes here; it's too crowded." —Yogi Berra

A reindeer walked into an ice cream shop, hopped up on a stool at the counter, and ordered a one-dollar hot butterscotch sundae.

When it arrived, he put a ten-dollar bill on the counter. But the waiter thought he wouldn't know anything about money and gave him only a dollar in change.

"You know," said the waiter, "we don't get many reindeer in here. In fact, I think you're the first one we've ever had."

"Well," the reindeer replied, "at nine dollars a sundae you probably won't get many more."

◉⊙◎

A well-known college football coach has been heard admitting, "I give the same half-time speech over and over. It works best when my players are better than the other coach's players."

◉⊙◎

A drought in Georgia began to affect how the churches in many communities had to conduct baptisms. The Baptists took up sprinkling, the Methodists used damp cloths, and the Presbyterians gave out rain checks.

What kind of bee is always dropping the football?
A fumblebee.

◉◉◉

Albert Einstein arrives at a party, introduces himself to the first person he sees, and asks, "What is your IQ?" to which the man answers, "Two hundred forty-one."

"That is wonderful!" responds Einstein. "We will talk about the mysteries of the universe."

Next Einstein introduces himself to a woman and asks, "What is your IQ?"

The lady answers, "One hundred forty-four."

"Excellent. We can discuss politics and current events. We will have much to talk about."

Einstein goes to another person and asks, "What is your IQ?"

The man answers, "Fifty-one."

Einstein responds, "How about them Cowboys?"

◉◉◉

Wife to friend: "It's Super Monday. Football season is over!"

What goes from Maine to Florida without moving?
The highway.

What can fall but will never break, and what can break but will never fall?
Night and day.

Four cars come to a four-way stop, each coming from either north, south, east, or west. It isn't clear who arrived first, so they all go at the same time. No one crashes, but all four cars successfully continue on their way. How is this possible?
They all made right-hand turns.

A woman was admiring her friend's newborn son. "He certainly favors his father," she said.

"You're right about that. Sleeps all the time, doesn't say anything, and doesn't have any hair."

⦿⦿⦿

A little boy went to the pet shop to buy a new food dish for his dog.

"Would you like to have your dog's name on the bowl?" the clerk asked.

"No, thanks. She can't read."

⦿⦿⦿

"Daryl, go wash your hands for dinner!" his mother commanded.

"But Mom, only one hand is dirty."

"Okay. If you think you can wash just that one, you're welcome to try."

A bright farm boy announced to his weathered old dad, "I've decided to go to medical school and study anesthesiology."

"I wouldn't, if I were you, boy," the father said. "By the time you graduate, they'll have a cure for it."

⊙⊙⊙

What kinds of people enjoy bad health?
Doctors.

⊙⊙⊙

A man returns from an overseas trip feeling very ill. He goes to see his doctor and is immediately rushed to the hospital to undergo a barrage of tests.

The man wakes up after the tests in a private room at the hospital. The phone by his bed rings.

"Hello. This is your doctor. We have received the results from your tests. We've found you have an extremely contagious virus."

"Oh, no!" cried the man. "What are you going to do?"

"Well," said the doctor, "we're going to put you on a diet of pizzas, pancakes, and pita bread."

"And that will cure me?" asked the man.

The doctor replied, "Well, no, but it's the only food we can slide under the door."

During a police academy class, the instructor began, "If you were called to an automobile accident with the chief of police in one car and the mayor in the other car. . .then suddenly you looked up to the top floor of a high-rise building across the street and saw a man standing on the railing. . .and then you looked down the street and saw several fire trucks were desperately fighting a fire in the courthouse. . .what would you do under these circumstances?"

One of the new recruits answered, "I'd remove my uniform and mingle with the crowd."

⊙⊙⊙

"My dad must be a pretty bad driver," said Brad.

"What do you mean?" asked Bret.

"I was with him when he got pulled over for speeding yesterday. The officer recognized him and wrote him out a season ticket."

⊙⊙⊙

A patrol officer chased down a speeder after a thirty-mile adventure on the interstate—only after the speeder had run out of gas.

"Congratulations," said the officer sarcastically. "You hit 163 miles per hour. I didn't think a little subcompact like that could give me such a run."

"And congratulations to you. I didn't think you could keep up."

A young husband and wife were about to buy an electric grill and put it on their credit card. They debated whether to select the economy model or the deluxe unit that had every imaginable convenience.

"Ah, let's go ahead and get the big one," said the husband.

"Yeah," said his wife. "It won't really cost us any more. We'll just have to pay a little longer."

◉⊙◎

Mary. "Know what? I never worry about money."
Barry: "How come?"
Mary: "What's the sense in worrying about something I don't have?"

◉⊙◎

"Just about the time you think you can make ends meet, someone moves the end." —Terry Hughes

In the first year of marriage, the man speaks and the woman listens. In the second year, the woman speaks and the man listens. In the third year, they both speak and the neighbors listen.

◎⊙◎

Quick Quips:

"A husband is someone who takes out the trash and gives the impression that he just cleaned the whole house."

"My wife keeps complaining I never listen to her—or something like that."

"Love is what happens when imagination overpowers common sense."

"Keep your eyes wide open before marriage—and half shut afterward."

"Marriage is like a violin—after the music stops, the strings are still attached."

"The most dangerous year in married life is the first, followed by the second, third, fourth, fifth. . . ."

◎⊙◎

What did the lovesick bull say to the cow?
"When I fall in love, it will be for heifer."

A professor asked a student to stay for a moment after class.

Holding the young man's assignment, the professor asked, "Did you write this poem by yourself?"

The student said, "Yes, I did—every word of it."

The professor extended his hand and said, "Well, then, I'm very glad to meet you, Mr. Wordsworth. I thought you had been dead for quite some time!"

◉⊙◎

Mom: "If you passed the test, why did your teacher fail you?"
Brad: "Because I passed it to Nate."

◉⊙◎

Who invented fractions?
Henry the 1/8.

Knock-knock.
Who's there?
Whittle.
Whittle who?
Whittle Orphan Annie.

◉⊙◎

Knock-knock.
Who's there?
Willoughby.
Willoughby who?
Willoughby my Valentine?

◉⊙◎

Knock-knock.
Who's there?
Albie.
Albie who?
Albie back—don't you forget it.

A little boy in Sunday school was asked what commandment he would break if he stayed home from Sunday school. He replied, "The fourth one: Keep the Sabbath Day holy."

Then he was asked what commandment he would break if he took his friend's bicycle. He replied, "The eighth: Do not steal."

Then he was asked what commandment he would break if he pulled his dog's tail. He hesitated, then said, "I don't know the number, but it goes like this: 'What God has joined together, let no man pull apart.'"

⊙⊙⊙

What kind of lights did Noah have on the ark?
Floodlights.

⊙⊙⊙

A just-out-of-seminary pastor was about to conduct his first wedding and was worried sick. An elderly preacher gave him some advice: "If you lose your place in the ceremony book or you forget your lines, start quoting scriptures until you find your place."

The wedding day came. And sure enough, the young man forgot where he was in the ritual. Unfortunately, the only verse he could think of was, "Father, forgive them, for they know not what they do."

What kind of ant is good at math?

An account-ant.

⊙⊙⊙

What do Paddington Bear and Winnie the Pooh pack for their holidays?

The bear essentials.

⊙⊙⊙

An affluent man paid twenty-five thousand dollars for an exotic bird for his mother.

"How did you like the bird?" he asked her later.

She responded, "It was delicious."

While in England on a summer European vacation, a neighbor sent post cards to everyone in her cul-de-sac back home in America. Her message read, "Fourth of July is not a big holiday here. The English are still a little testy."

◉◉◉

"Do you have a card?" one businesswoman asked another.

Cards were exchanged, and the first woman looked puzzled. "There's no name on it."

The second woman glanced around furtively. "That's for tax purposes. I need to maintain my anonymity."

◉◉◉

Amanda: "Daddy, does money really talk?"
Dad: "No, honey. It goes without saying."

A man vacationing in Italy happened to be in the bathroom of his hotel suite when a devastating earthquake shook the building to its frame. Pictures dropped from the walls. Plaster fell from the ceilings. Screams from adjoining rooms and sirens from the streets below filled the air.

Members of the hotel staff hurried from room to room to check on their guests. When they arrived at the American's suite, they found him cowering by the toilet. "I swear," he cried, holding up his hands and shaking his head in disbelief, "all I did was pull the chain!"

◉ ◉ ◉

An American couple visiting Ireland watched a truck pass by, loaded with turf.

"What a great idea!" the wife exclaimed. "That's what we should do with our grass—send it out to be trimmed."

◉ ◉ ◉

Frank: "We just returned from vacation in Switzerland."
Al: "Berne?"
Frank: "No, froze."

Toward the end of a particularly trying round of golf, Troy was the picture of frustration. He'd hit too many fat shots. Finally he blurted out to his caddie, "I'd move heaven and earth to break a hundred on this course."

"Try heaven," replied the caddie. "You've already moved most of the earth."

⊙⊙⊙

If you live in Green Bay, Wisconsin, how do you keep bears out of your backyard?
Put up goalposts.

⊙⊙⊙

Practical Camping Tips:

When using a public campground, a tuba placed on your picnic table will keep the sites on either side of you vacant.

When smoking fish, never inhale.

You'll never be lost if you remember that moss always grows on the north side of your compass.

You can duplicate the warmth of a down-filled sleeping bag by climbing into a plastic garbage bag with several geese.

Turn old socks into high-fiber beef jerky by smoking them over an open fire.

When camping, always wear a long-sleeved shirt. It gives you something to wipe your nose on.

A hot rock placed in your sleeping bag will keep your feet warm. A hot enchilada works almost as well, but the cheese sticks between your toes.

A woman says to you, "Everything I say to you is a lie." Is she telling you the truth or is she lying?

She's lying. Even though she's lying when she says "everything" she says is a lie, some of the things she says can be a lie, and this is one of them.

⊙⊙⊚

How can the statement "Four is half of five" be true?

If four is written in roman numerals (IV), then it is half of F(IV)E.

⊙⊙⊚

When full, I can point the way, but when empty, nothing moves me. I have two skins—one outside and one inside. What am I?

A glove.

A tenth-grade boy came home with a poor report card. As he handed it to his father, he asked, "What do you think is wrong, Dad, my heredity or my environment?"

○⊙◎

Pastor George and wife Sally brought their new bundle of joy home to the parsonage. Days went by with Sally watching every move baby Georgie made while George Sr. busied himself with heavy global and theological thoughts. Naturally the care began to take its toll on Sally, causing her husband to gallantly announce; "I know you're having a lot of trouble with Georgie, dear, but keep in mind, 'the hand that rocks the cradle is the hand that rules the world.'"

Sally replied, "How about taking over the world for a few hours while I go shopping?"

○⊙◎

"I heard you and your wife arguing last night," a man remarked to his newly married neighbor. "Honeymoon over?"

"Not really. It's just that when it comes to some things, I won't change my opinion and she won't change the subject."

What kind of computer would you find in the Garden of Eden?
Adam's Apple.

⊙⊙⊚

A computer technician was called to the school to repair a computer. He wasn't able to find a close parking spot, so he left his car in a no-parking zone and placed a note on his windshield saying, "Scott Brown, Computer Technician, Working inside the Building."

He was finished working within an hour, and when he returned to his car, he found a ticket with a note that read, "David Jackson, Police Officer, Working outside the Building."

⊙⊙⊚

What did the computer programmer say to the waiter?
"May I see a pull-down menu, please?"

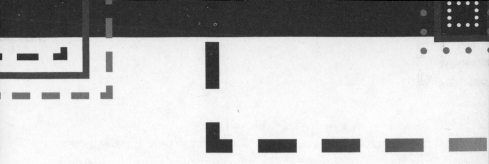

Knock-knock.
Who's there?
Astronaut.
Astronaut who?
Astronaut what your country can do for you, but what you
can do for your country.

◉◉◉

What's an astronaut's favorite sandwich?
Launch meat.

◉◉◉

I am strongest when you view me whole, but I am often
found in other shapes. I move the oceans with my incredible
strength, and an explorer with a name like 'powerful bicep'
was the first to walk on me. What am I?
The moon.

A passenger train is creeping along very slowly. Finally it comes to a halt. A passenger sees a conductor walking by outside.

"Can you tell me what's going on?" she yells out the window.

"There's a cow on the tracks!" answers the conductor.

Ten minutes later, the train resumes its slow pace.

Within five minutes, however, it stops once again.

The woman sees the same conductor walking past the window again.

She leans out and yells, "What happened? Did we catch up with the cow again?"

⊙⊙⊙

What has wheels and flies?
A garbage truck.

⊙⊙⊙

A stranger frantically ran up to a farmer's house, pounded his fist on the door, and demanded, "Where's the nearest railroad station, and what time's the next train to the city?"

The farmer came to the screen door and thought a moment. "Cut through my back hayfield, and you ought to reach the crossroads station in time for the 5:40. Actually, if my bull spots you, I expect you'll make the 5:15."

A professor was discussing a particularly complicated concept. A premed student rudely interrupted him and asked, "Why do we have to learn this pointless information?"

"To save lives," the professor responded quickly and continued the lecture.

A few minutes later, the same student spoke up again. "So how does physics save lives?" he inquired.

"It keeps people like you out of medical school," replied the professor.

◉◉◉

A man came home from the doctor's office, and his wife asked how he had checked out.

"Hmph," the man said disgustedly. "He told me I'm either forty pounds too heavy or four inches too short."

◉◉◉

Aboard an airplane, Mr. Wilson overheard the flight attendant address his seatmate as "Dr. Adams."

"So, you're a doctor, eh?" Mr. Wilson said. "I've been meaning to ask one of you fellas about a pain I have in my right side."

"I'm afraid I wouldn't be able to help you," the other passenger said pleasantly. "My training is in the area of homiletics."

Mr. Wilson was silent for a while. Then he asked, "Homiletics—is that fatal?"

"Come on up and join the army of the Lord!" invited the preacher at the close of a Methodist revival service.

"Already joined," piped an impatient voice from the congregation.

"Oh? Where did you join?" asked the preacher.

"First Baptist Church, two years ago."

The preacher shook his head. "Mercy! You're not in the army—you've joined the navy!"

◉ ◉ ◉

Why was the sailor afraid of geometry?
He heard the Bermuda Triangle will make you disappear.

◉ ◉ ◉

Why did the army begin drafting babies?
It was trying to build up the infantry.

A customer was continually bothering the waiter in a restaurant. First, he asked that the air-conditioning be turned up because he was too hot; then he asked that it be turned down because he was too cold. That continued for about half an hour.

The waiter was very patient, walking back and forth and never once getting angry. Finally, a second customer asked why they just didn't ask the man to leave.

"Oh, I don't mind," said the waiter calmly. "We don't even have an air conditioner."

⊙⊙⊙

While eating in an expensive restaurant, a patron overhead the gentleman at the next table ask the waitress to pack the leftovers for their dog. The gentleman's young son then exclaimed, "Whoopee! We're going to get a dog!"

⊙⊙⊙

Knock-knock.
Who's there?
Moose.
Moose who?
*Urrrp. . .*moose be something I ate.

Teacher: "If you have fifteen potatoes and must divide them equally among five people, how would you do it?"
Shelly: "I'd mash them."

⊙⊙⊙

An English teacher kept this wood-carved sign above her classroom door: DEPARTMENT OF REDUNDANCY DEPARTMENT.

⊙⊙⊙

History According to Students:

Queen Victoria was the longest queen. She sat on a thorn for sixty-three years. Her reclining years and finally the end of her life were exemplary of a great personality. Her death was the final event which ended her reign. The sun never set on the British Empire because the British Empire is in the east and the sun sets in the west.

The nineteenth century was a time of many great inventions and thoughts. The invention of the steamboat caused a network of rivers to spring up. Samuel Morse invented a code of telepathy. Louis Pasteur discovered a cure for rabbis. Charles Darwin was a naturalist who wrote the *Organ of the Species.*

The children's Sunday school department was undertaking a study of the book of Proverbs. To illustrate what proverbs are, Miss Daisy collected the first phrase of a bunch of traditional ones and asked the children to creatively complete them. Here are some results:

Better to be safe than. . .punch a fifth-grader.
Strike while the. . .bug is close.
Don't bite the hand that. . .looks dirty.
The pen is mightier than the. . .pigs.
A penny saved. . .is not very much.
Children should be seen and not. . .spanked or grounded.

◉⊙◉

The preacher told me the other day I should be thinking about the Hereafter.

I told him, "I do, all the time. No matter where I am—in the parlor, upstairs, in the kitchen, or in the basement. I'm always asking myself, 'Now, what am I here after?'"

◉⊙◉

"When did Adam and Eve eat the apple?" a Sunday school teacher asked.

"In the summertime," answered a student.

"Why, Brenda, how do you know that?" the teacher asked.

"Well, we all know it was just before the fall."

Knock-knock.
Who's there?
Aardvark.
Aardvark who?
"Aardvark a million miles for one of your smiles."

⊙⊙⊙

Knock-knock.
Who's there?
Amish.
Amish who?
Amish you very much.

⊙⊙⊙

Knock-knock.
Who's there?
Churchill.
Churchill who?
Churchill be the best place for a summer wedding.

Why was the centipede dropped from the insect football team?
He took too long to put his boots on.

◉⊙◎

There was a preacher who was trying to sell his horse. A potential buyer came to the church for a test ride. "Before you begin," the preacher said, "you need to know there is something special about this horse. You have to say, 'Praise the Lord,' to make it go and 'Amen' to make it stop."

So the man mounted the horse and said, "Praise the Lord," and the horse started to trot. The man again said, "Praise the Lord," and the horse started to gallop. Soon he saw a cliff ahead. In his fright, he yelled, "Whoa, stop!" He then remembered the term the horse understood. "Amen!"

The horse stopped just inches from the edge of the cliff. The man leaned back in the saddle, wiped the sweat from his brow, and said, "Praise the Lord!"

◉⊙◎

Which big cat should you never play a board game with?
A cheetah.

A news-editing professor, grading the results of a proofreading test, was devastated to notice this sentence in his own instructions: "Read slowly and carefully to sure nothing missing."

◉⊙◎

In northern Maine, they say there are two seasons: winter and roadwork.

◉⊙◎

The customer wanted to buy a chicken and the butcher had only one in stock. He weighed it and said, "This one's a beauty. That will be $4.25."

"Oh, but that isn't quite large enough," said the customer. The butcher put the chicken back in the refrigerator, rolled it around on the ice several times, then placed it back on the scale again.

"This one is $5.50," he said, adding his thumb to the weight.

"Oh, that's great!" said the customer. "I'll take both of them, please."

How to Annoy Your Man on Super Bowl Sunday:

Take the batteries out of all the remote controls.
Show a sudden interest in every aspect of the game. Especially
    have him define the offside rule several times.
Plug in a boom box and do your Dancerobics routine.
Decide it's time to dust the house, starting with a particularly
    good dusting of the television set right at kickoff.
Invite your mother over for the game.
Get a *Better Homes & Gardens* magazine, sit in the room, and
    read extra-good passages aloud.
Invite your friends over for a Pampered Chef party.
It's your night out with the girls; leave the kids home with him!

◉⊙◎

"I thought I told you to keep an eye on your cousin!" the
mother impatiently barked. "Where is he?"

"Well," her son replied thoughtfully, "if he knows as much
about canoeing as he thinks he does, he's out canoeing. If he
knows as little as I think he does, he's out swimming."

◉⊙◎

Ella: "I just adore tennis. I could play like this forever."
Mark: "You will, if you don't take lessons."

You move to an island in the middle of a lake. This lake is in a remote part of the state and there has never been a bridge connecting the island to the mainland. Every day a tractor and wagon gives rides around the island to tourists. Puzzled as to how the tractor had gotten onto the island, you ask around. You find out that the tractor was not built on the island and was not transported to the island by boat or by air. How did the tractor get to the island?

The owner waited until winter and then drove the tractor over on the frozen lake.

◉◉◉

A wee man in a little red coat.
Staff in his hand, and stone in his throat.
What am I?

A cherry.

◉◉◉

What kind of snake is good at math?

An adder.

The first grade teacher on the opening day of school asked a student if he knew how to count.

"Yes," he beamed. "I learned from my daddy."

"Let me hear you count from five to ten."

The child did as he was asked.

"Now, do you know what comes after ten?"

"Jack!"

⊙⊙⊙

She: "Our problem is that we're just not communicating."

He: "I don't wanna discuss it."

⊙⊙⊙

A mother peeked in to hear her child say his prayers at bedtime. The boy had been in a fussy mood, and his sentences came in mumbled fragments.

"I can't hear what you're saying," his mother gently admonished.

"I'm not praying to you," the child pouted.

"I've sat at this bench for twelve years," the judge said, "and this is the fifth time you've been brought before me on disorderly conduct charges. Aren't you ashamed?"

The defendant muttered to her lawyer, "He can't get a promotion, and he takes it out on us."

A judge admonished a defendant, "Are you aware how close this came to being a murder trial and not an attempted murder trial?"

"I believe so, Your Honor. The primary difference, as I see it, is that the rotten scoundrel lived."

Judge: "How do you plead?"
Defendant: "What's the evidence?"

A teacher approached young Horace shaking her head. "Your handwriting is absolutely unreadable," she said. "You're going to have a tough time in life, if no one can read what you write. The only option I see is for you to become a doctor."

◉☉◎

"I really appreciate your coming out to our house this late at night," remarked a sick patient.

"No problem," said the doctor. "I had to come see Mr. Oaks just down the road, anyway. This way I can kill two birds with one stone."

◉☉◎

When is the best time to make a dentist appointment? *Tooth-hurty.*

What did King George say when he heard about the rebellious American colonies?
"How revolting!"

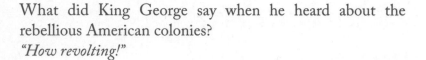

"What do you think was the most important invention in all of history?" the teacher asked her class.

"The automobile," answered one student.

"The airplane," answered the second.

"The nuclear submarine," answered the third.

"The credit card," answered the fourth.

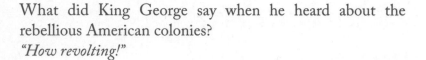

If King Henry VIII were alive today, what would he be most famous for?
Extreme old age.

Three eligible widows were discussing several eligible widowers in their church.

"Now George is a nice man," remarked one, "and he really doesn't look sixty."

Another was far less impressed by George's youthful appearance. "Well," she said, "he used to look sixty."

◉ ◉ ◉

A ninety-five-year-old gentleman entered a life insurance office and told the agent he wanted to take out a three hundred thousand dollar whole-life policy.

"But you're simply too old," the agent said after a moment's consideration. "No insurance company would start a new policy on a ninety-five-year-old client."

"Sonny boy," the applicant steamed, "are you aware of the mortality demographics within the United States of America?"

"Why, yes, sir. I believe I know the statistics pretty well."

"What percentage of the population is known to die between the ages of 90 and 120?"

"Er, something less than 5 percent..."

"Then what, exactly, is your problem with my age bracket?"

The agent wrote the policy.

◉ ◉ ◉

Two children were caught in mischief by their grandmother. Happily, she chose not to punish them. "I remember being young once, too," she mused.

"Gee, Grandma," said one of the children, wide-eyed. "You sure have an incredible memory!"

What kind of fish should you use to make a peanut butter sandwich?
Jellyfish.

⊙⊙⊙

What is lighter than the material it is made of and keeps most of itself hidden from sight?
An iceberg.

⊙⊙⊙

A fisherman was bragging about a monster of a fish he caught. A friend broke in and chided, "Yeah, I saw a picture of that fish, and he was all of six inches long."

"Yeah," said the proud fisherman. "But after battling for three hours, a fish can lose a lot of weight."

Teacher: "If I cut a steak in two, then cut the halves in two, what do I get?"

Student: "Quarters."

Teacher: "Very good. And what would I get if I cut it again?"

Student: "Eighths."

Teacher: "Great job! And if I cut it again?"

Student: "Sixteenths."

Teacher: "Wonderful! And again?"

Student: "Hamburger."

◉◉◉

Three magic words for schoolteachers: *June, July,* and *August*.

◉◉◉

A middle school was faced with a problem. After putting on their lipstick, some girls would pucker up and press their lips against the bathroom mirrors, leaving many lip prints.

One day, the principal thought of a way to put an end to this problem. She called all the girls to the bathroom and had the custodian meet them there. She explained to the girls that the lip prints were causing extra work for the custodian because he had to clean the mirrors every day.

To prove to the girls how difficult it was for him to clean the mirrors, she asked the custodian to clean one of the mirrors. He took out a long-handled brush, dipped it into the nearest toilet, and thoroughly scrubbed the mirror.

No lip prints were seen on the mirrors again.

Knock-knock.
Who's there?
Bless.
Bless who?
Thanks, but I didn't sneeze.

◉◉◉

Knock-knock.
Who's there?
Spell.
Spell who?
W-H-O!

◉◉◉

Knock-knock.
Who's there?
Toodle.
Toodle who?
Toodle-oo to you, too.

A clock-watching parishioner couldn't refrain from commenting to the minister after a church service, "Your sermons begin well enough, but why do you make them so long? I'm afraid a lot of folks lose interest."

The minister had a ready reply: "Sermonettes make for Christianettes."

◉ ◉ ◉

Pastor: "How did the assistant pastor's sermon go Sunday?"
Church Member: "It was a poor sermon. Nothing in it at all."

(Upon seeing the assistant pastor:)

Pastor: "How did it go Sunday morning?"
Assistant: "Excellently. I didn't have time to prepare anything myself, so I preached one of your sermons."

◉ ◉ ◉

A preacher spoke twenty minutes on Isaiah, twenty minutes on Ezekiel, twenty minutes on Jeremiah, and twenty minutes on Daniel. Then he announced, "We have now come to the twelve minor prophets. What place will I give Hosea?"

A man on the back row shouted out, "I'm leaving! Give Hosea my place!"

What do you give a deer with an upset stomach?
Elk-a-seltzer.

⊙⊙⊙

Two serious fishermen went fishing one summer day. For four hours neither of them moved a muscle. Then the one up forward became a bit restless.

"Will you stop that?" grumbled his companion. "That's the second time you've shifted your feet in twenty minutes. Did you come out here to fish or dance?"

⊙⊙⊙

Upon entering a little country store, a stranger noticed a sign reading: DANGER! BEWARE OF DOG, posted on the glass door.

Inside, he noticed a harmless old hound dog asleep on the floor beside the counter. He asked the store manager, "Is that the dog folks are supposed to beware of?"

"Yup, sure is," he replied.

The stranger couldn't help but smile in amusement. "That certainly doesn't appear to be a dangerous dog to me. Why did you post that sign?"

"Well," the owner replied, "before I posted that sign, people kept tripping over him."

Did you hear about the latest government study on aging? It cost 240 million dollars and provided compelling evidence that the average American is growing older.

Name of a twenty-four-hour oriental restaurant: "Wok 'Round the Clock."

Humorous Headlines:

Rash of Accidents Keeps EMT Crews Hopping
Dinner Theater Relies on Seasoned Cast
Slain Youth Found Alive
Cars Collide; One Charged with Abusive Language

Golfer: "Notice any improvement since last year?"
Caddy: "Polished your clubs, didn't you?"

Two men were warming up to play tennis when one man noticed that the other had bruised shins. "Those look like they're in pretty bad shape. You play hockey, too?"

"No," replied the other man, "bridge. I just trumped my wife's ace."

A Limerick

A javelin thrower called Vicky
Found the grip of her javelin sticky.
When it came to the throw,
She couldn't let go,
Making judging the distance quite tricky.

If a bungalow is red and everything in it is red, what color are the stairs?
Bungalows don't have stairs.

⊙⊙⊚

At night they come without being called
And move around without being walled.
But at the very first sign of light,
They disappear back into the night.
What are they?
Stars.

⊙⊙⊚

How many legs does a horse have?
Six. It has forelegs in the front and two legs in the back.

At 3:00 in the morning, a young wife shook her husband awake.

"What is it?" he asked groggily.

"The baby," she reminded him.

The husband sat up and listened a full minute. "But I don't hear her crying," he protested.

"I know. It's your turn to go see why not."

"I think the older my grandpa gets," a girl remarked to a friend, "the farther he had to walk to school when he was my age."

Two mothers were comparing child-rearing notes. "I just can't seem to get my children's attention," said one. "They stay mesmerized in front of the television set. I say things to them and call for them, and they're oblivious to every word."

"Try sitting in an easy chair and looking like you're relaxed," said the other. "That gets my children's attention without fail."

The firm's administrator really was taken by the character of the job applicant, but she strongly suspected the woman was past retirement age.

"On your application," the administrator remarked tactfully, "I see your birthday is the same as my mother's: September 6. May I ask what year?"

"Every year," came the stoic reply.

◉◉◎

A teenaged boy had searched for a job long and hard and was devastated to be turned down for a position working the counter at a fast-food restaurant. The reason, explained the manager, was the boy's illiteracy.

Undaunted, he began doing people's yard work, then learned the basics of routine landscaping and ultimately acquired a local reputation as a knowledgeable, professional landscaper. He opened his own shrub nursery, which led to a chain of nurseries. By age thirty-five he was the town's wealthiest citizen—and remained illiterate.

"Just imagine where you might be," his wife mused one day, "if you could read and write."

◉◉◎

A carpenter fell two stories and landed with a thud on his back.

"What happened?" asked a coworker, rushing to his side.

"I'm not sure," the victim said. "I just got here."

The transatlantic flight to England was halfway across when the pilot came on the intercom with a casual message to the passengers: "You may have noticed a slight change in the sound of the engines. That's because we've had to shut down Engine Two temporarily. There's no cause for concern; we have three more engines in fine condition. But there'll be a slight delay. Our expected time of arrival has been changed from 2:14 p.m. to 2:45 p.m. Sorry for any inconvenience that may cause."

An hour later the pilot was back on the intercom, chuckling softly. "Folks, this is the first time I've ever experienced this, and I never thought it would happen, but we seem to have lost power in Engine Four. No problem in terms of safety, but we'll have a further delay. We now expect to arrive at Heathrow International at 3:30 p.m."

And a little while later he was back at the mike, still trying to sound reassuring but with an edge in his voice. "You won't believe this, but Engine One seems to be on the blink, and we've decided it's wise to shut it down. This is a weird situation, but not really alarming. We can easily finish the flight with one engine, although we'll be flying substantially slower. We now anticipate arriving around 4:25."

One passenger turned to another and mumbled, "If that last engine goes out, it'll be next Tuesday till we get to England."

◉ ⊙ ◎

"Were you in complete control of the car at the time of the accident?" the judge asked the defendant.

"No, Your Honor. My wife was with me."

◉ ⊙ ◎

How does a skunk's car run?
On fumes.

Little Johnny and his family lived in the country and, as a result, seldom had guests for dinner. On this particular evening, he was eager to help his mom when Dad brought two guests home from work.

When the dinner was nearly over, Little Johnny went to the kitchen and proudly carried in the first piece of apple pie, giving it to his father, who passed it on to a guest.

Little Johnny came in with a second piece of pie and gave it to his father, who again passed it on to a guest.

This was too much for Little Johnny, who said, "It's no use, Dad, the pieces are all the same size."

◉⊙◎

Jeff: "Why are you so eager to meet the right woman, settle down, and get married?"
Mike: "So I can stop dieting."

◉⊙◎

Why did the fraction want to go on a diet?
It wanted to reduce.

Police were investigating a break-in:

"Didn't you hear any strange noises next door last evening?" they asked one neighbor.

"We couldn't hear anything. Their dog was barking too loud."

⊚⊙⊚

Knock-knock.
Who's there?
CD.
CD who?
CD badge? This is the police. Open up!

⊚⊙⊚

A group of detectives was lounging around the police station.

"I can't believe it," said one detective. "We haven't had a thing to investigate for the past two days. No shootings, no robberies, no embezzlements, no nothing."

"Just give folks a little time," said a partner.

Why is the law of gravity untrustworthy?
It will always let you down.

⊙ ⊙ ⊙

Son: "Dad, I'm tired of doing homework."
Father: "Hard work never killed anyone, you know."
Son: "I know. But I don't want to be the first!"

⊙ ⊙ ⊙

What numbers are always wandering around?
Roamin' numerals.

Knock-knock.
Who's there?
Renata.
Renata who?
Renata milk, may I borrow some?

Knock-knock.
Who's there?
Aikido.
Aikido who?
Aikido you not.

Knock-knock.
Who's there?
Water skier.
Water skier who?
Water skier'd of, I'm harmless!

Day 332

If Samuel Clemens was cloned, we would have identical Twains.

⊙⊙⊙

You do know what would have happened if it had been three wise women instead of men, don't you? They would have asked for directions, arrived on time, helped deliver the baby, cleaned the stable, made a casserole, and brought disposable diapers as a gift!

⊙⊙⊙

As a special Youth Week project, a university group was asked to list ways the Bible may have been different if it had been written by fellow students. These are a few they came up with:

Loaves and fishes would have been replaced by pizza and chips.

Ten Commandments are actually five, but because they are double-spaced and written in a large font, they look like ten.

Forbidden fruit would have been eaten only because it wasn't dining hall food.

Paul's letter to the Romans would become Paul's e-mail to the Romans.

Reason Cain killed Abel—they were roommates.

Place where the end of the world occurs—not the Plains of Armageddon, but Finals.

Reason why Moses and followers wandered in the desert for forty years—they didn't want to ask directions and look like freshmen.

Tower of Babel blamed for foreign language requirement.

Instead of creating the world in six days and resting on the seventh, God would have put it off until the night before it was due and then pulled an all-nighter and hoped no one noticed.

"Why is your dog growling at me while I'm eating?" Dave asked Steve. "Does he want me to give him some food?"

"No," said Steve. "He's just mad because you're eating off his favorite plate."

◉ ⊙ ◎

Jeweler: "Hello, 9-1-1. I own a jewelry store and an elephant just walked in, sucked up all the jewelry with his trunk, and ran out."

Police: "Can you give me a description?"

Jeweler: "Not really—he had a nylon stocking over his head."

◉ ⊙ ◎

A pig went to the bank for a loan to buy some trinkets for his new house.

"Hi, my name is Mr. Paddywhack," one of the bankers said. "How can I help you?"

When the pig explained, the banker frowned and said, "I'm sorry, but we never lend money to animals."

"Please," requested the pig. "I promise I'll pay it back."

"Perhaps you had better speak to the manager," insisted Mr. Paddywhack.

A few minutes later, the manager appeared, and the pig again pleaded, "Please, all I need is a little money to buy some trinkets."

"I told him we don't lend money to livestock," the banker retorted.

"Oh, for goodness' sake!" exclaimed the manager, throwing his hands up in the air. "It's a knickknack, Paddywhack, give the hog a loan!"

Bloopers:

"If across-the-board salary raises are not approved for District Five teachers, several have threatened to abandon their pests."

"The refreshment table was superintended by Mrs. Smith, overflowing with sweets and sandwiches."

"Mrs. Jones will sink two numbers. She will be accompanied by the choir."

Paper-clipped special in a lunch menu: SOUTHERN-STYLE MANHATTAN CLAM CHOWDER.

◉ ◉ ◉

"Do you take this woman for your wedded wife?" the minister asked the nervous bridegroom. "For better or worse, for richer, for poorer, in sickness or. . ."

"Just a minute, Pastor!" interrupted the bride. "Stop now, or you'll talk him right out of it."

◉ ◉ ◉

A professor was turned down on his application to a new college post. "Not enough published work," said the dean. "You have only one book to your credit."

"Are you aware that God Himself has only one book to His credit?"

"Then He needn't apply here."

What part of your body is helpful during the Boston Marathon?
A runny nose.

Definitions:

Duffer: A golfing enthusiast who shouts "Fore!" takes five strokes, then writes three on the scorecard.
Pro Football Coach: A man who's willing to lay down his players' lives in order to win.
Quarterback: A nominal refund.
Refugee: An official at a professional wrestling match.

Knock-knock.
Who's there?
Pharaoh.
Pharaoh who?
Pharaoh foul, this is baseball.

What is the moon worth?
Four quarters.

One morning, a man is preparing to leave town, but first stops by his office to pick up his messages. While he is at the office, the night watchman stops him and says, "Sir, don't go on this trip. I had a dream last night that the plane will crash and you will die!" The man decides to cancel his trip. Just as the watchman predicted, the plane crashes and no one survives. The very next morning, the man rewards the watchman with one thousand dollars, but then fires him. Why would he fire the watchman who saved his life?
The "night" watchman was fired for sleeping on the job!

What appears once in every minute, twice in every moment, but not once in a billion years?
The letter M.

You know you're a mother when you're up each night un-til 10:00 p.m., vacuuming, dusting, wiping, washing, drying, loading, unloading, shopping, cooking, driving, flushing, iron-ing, sweeping, picking up, changing sheets, changing diapers, bathing, helping with homework, paying bills, budgeting, clip-ping coupons, folding clothes, putting to bed, dragging out of bed, brushing, chasing, buckling, feeding, swinging, playing ball, bike riding, pushing trucks, cuddling dolls, rollerblading, catching, blowing bubbles, running sprinklers, sliding, tak-ing walks, coloring, crafting, jumping rope, raking, trimming, planting, edging, mowing, gardening, painting, and walking/feeding the dog. You get up at 5:30 a.m., and you have no time to eat, sleep, drink, or go to the bathroom, and yet—you still manage to gain ten pounds.

☻☺☻

It had been a very long day, and the mother had had it up to the eyebrows with problems and commotion.

"If you don't turn down that rap CD," she shrieked to her teenaged son, "I'll go absolutely bananas!"

"It may be too late," her son said sheepishly. "I turned it off about fifteen minutes ago."

☻☺☻

Mrs. Laird: "Do you ever wake up grouchy in the morning?"
Mrs. Baird: "No, I usually let him just get up whenever he's ready."

A computer salesman was trying to talk a customer into buying a high-speed, high-priced, brand-new, barely tested machine.

"But the other one has all I really need," she objected. "I don't care if the technology is six months old. I'm only going to use it for word processing. What's wrong with it?"

"Speed," said the clerk, shaking his head. "The new machine reboots much, much faster."

A man passing by in the aisle whispered, "And much more often."

◉◉◉

What's a computer's worst health fear?
The slipped disk.

◉◉◉

At the beginning of math class, the teacher asked, "Timmy, what are 3 and 6 and 27 and 45?"

Timmy quickly answered, "NBC, CBS, ESPN, and the Cartoon Network!"

Two jocks were taking a break in the gym.

"What's your weight?"

"About 190."

"Gained a little, haven't you?"

"More'n a little. I only weighed 8 pounds 5 ounces when I was born."

⊚ ⊙ ⊚

A surgeon asked a patient, "Could you afford an operation if I thought it was necessary?"

The patient replied, "Would you think it was necessary if I couldn't afford one?"

⊚ ⊙ ⊚

Dr. James wasn't at all pleased to discover Mrs. Bryan had come to him for a third opinion before agreeing to surgery. "You should have come to me to begin with," he stated. "Who did you see first?"

"Dr. Morgan."

"Well, I suppose there are worse GPs, but the man has no vision. What did he tell you?"

"He said I need surgery, but I should get another doctor's opinion."

"And who did you see next?"

"Dr. Lattimore."

"The imbecile! That man's knowledge of medicine could be contained in a thimble. His advice is totally worthless. What on earth did he tell you?"

"He told me to come see you."

Two boys were entering the classroom on exam day. "I don't care if it is unconstitutional," said one. "I'm saying a prayer before this one."

◉⊙◎

Cindy: "I've been calling and calling the city council to do something about those terrible potholes! After months of badgering, the council finally took action."
Mindy: "And now are the potholes filled?"
Cindy: "No, now the city council has an unlisted number!"

◉⊙◎

A caveman explained to his clan the reasons they needed to establish an elected government. The tribe listened patiently as he talked. Then another man stood up.

"Let me get this straight," he said. "You want me and the other guys to go out every day, hunt dangerous mastodons and saber-toothed tigers while you sleep late inside the cave, give you part of the food, let you dictate to us where and when we're entitled to hunt—and this is for the good of us all?"

What kind of cheese did Frankenstein like?
Muenster.

⊙⊙⊙

Knock-knock.
Who's there?
Yoda.
Yoda who?
Yoda best!

⊙⊙⊙

Why wouldn't Cinderella give her prince the time of day?
Because it was midnight.

Day
342

The following is an explanation of the school homework policy for the average student: "Students should not spend more than ninety minutes per night on an assignment. This time should be budgeted in the following manner if the student desires to achieve moderate to good grades in his/her classes:

Eleven minutes looking for the assignment.
Fourteen minutes calling a friend for the assignment.
Seventeen minutes explaining why the teacher is so unfair.
Nine minutes in the bathroom.
Twelve minutes getting a snack.
Eight minutes checking the *TV Guide*.
Nine minutes telling parents that the teacher never explained the assignment.
Ten minutes sitting at the kitchen table waiting for Mom or Dad to do the assignment."

⊙⊙⊙

The best part of going back to school is seeing all your friends. The worst part is that your teachers won't let you talk to them.

⊙⊙⊙

Father: "You have four Ds and a C on your report card!"
Son: "Maybe I concentrated too much on the one subject."

Knock-knock.
Who's there?
Sarah.
Sarah who?
Sarah a florist in the house?

◉⦿◎

Knock-knock.
Who's there?
Quacker.
Quacker who?
Quacker 'nother bad joke and I'm outta here!

◉⦿◎

Knock-knock.
Who's there?
State Highway Patrol.
State Highway Patrol who?
Better not ask questions!

Church choir members were putting on a car wash to raise money for their annual tour. They made a large sign which read, Car Wash for Choir Trip.

On the given Saturday, business was terrific, but by two o'clock the skies clouded and the rain poured, and there were hardly any customers.

Finally one of the girl washers had an idea. She printed a large cardboard poster that read, We Wash and God Rinses. Business boomed!

◉⊙◎

A family is greeting its pastor after the service. Junior looks up and declares, "My dad says my mom is a pagan because she serves burnt offerings for dinner."

◉⊙◎

Bobby's parents tried their best to keep him from acting up during the morning worship hour, but they were losing the battle. Finally the father picked up the little fellow and walked sternly up the aisle to apply a little discipline. Just before reaching the foyer, little Bobby called loudly to the congregation, "Pray for me! Pray for me!"

A tourist was fishing off the coast of Florida when his boat capsized. He could swim, but he was afraid there might be alligators, so he hung onto the side of the overturned boat.

Spotting an old beachcomber standing on the shore, the tourist called, "Are there any alligators around here?"

"Nah," the man hollered back. "They haven't been around here for years!"

Feeling safe, the tourist began swimming toward shore. About halfway there, he asked the guy, "How'd they get rid of the gators?"

"They didn't do anything," answered the beachcomber. "The sharks got 'em all."

◉◉◉

Hunter 1: "Look! Here's some bear tracks!"
Hunter 2: "Great. I'll go see where he came from, and you go see where he went."

◉◉◉

Why do dinosaurs have wrinkles in their knees?
They stayed in the swimming pool too long.

Senator: "The United States has made a lot of progress over the past hundred years or so."

Reporter: "It sure has. President Washington couldn't tell a lie, and now every politician in Washington can."

⊙⊙⊙

"Aren't you ready yet, dear?" an impatient husband asked his wife.

"In a minute!" his wife shouted in exasperation. "I've told you fifty times already."

⊙⊙⊙

Churchman Bill Keane, creator of the popular *Family Circus* comic strip, tells of a time when he was penciling-in one of his cartoons and his son Jeffy asked, "Daddy, how do you know what to draw?"

Keane answered, "God tells me."

Then Jeffy innocently responded, "Then why do you keep erasing parts of it?"

The first rule of watching basketball on television: Watch only the last two minutes. Nothing much happens until then, and those two minutes will last a half hour.

⊙⊙⊙

Knock-knock.
Who's there?
Howard.
Howard who?
Howard you like to play shortstop?

⊙⊙⊙

A little boy was overheard talking to himself as he strutted through his backyard, carrying a ball and bat and shouting, "I'm the greatest hitter in the world!" Then he tossed the ball into the air, swung at it, and missed.

"Strike one!" he yelled. Undaunted, he picked up the ball and repeated, "I'm the greatest hitter in the world!" When it came down, he swung again and missed. "Strike two!" he cried.

The boy paused a moment, examined the ball, spit on his hands, adjusted his hat, and repeated, "I'm the greatest hitter in the world!"

Again he tossed the ball up and swung at it. He missed. "Strike three!"

"Wow!" he exclaimed. "I'm the greatest *pitcher* in the world!"

I come in different shapes and sizes.
Part of me has curves; part of me is straight.
You can put me anywhere you like,
but there is only one right place for me.
What am I?
A jigsaw puzzle.

⊙⊙⊙

What would you get if you crossed the Indian Ocean with chili powder?
Heat waves.

⊙⊙⊙

Do you say, "Eight and four is eleven" or, "Eight and four are eleven"?
Neither. Eight and four are twelve.

Day 349

Walt: "I just don't know what to get my wife for our anniversary."

John: "Why don't you ask her what she wants?"

Walt: "Oh, no! That would cost too much."

⊙⊙⊙

A man was arguing with his wife over which gender shows better judgment. Ultimately, she gave in. "You're right. Men exercise better judgment, and the two of us are living proof of it, aren't we? I mean, you chose me for a wife, and I chose you for a husband."

⊙⊙⊙

Mom and Dad were getting started with Saturday chores when their child came out into the yard.

"Why don't you go across the street and ask how old Mrs. Wells is this morning?" Dad suggested.

The child dutifully crossed the street, greeted their neighbor three doors down, and asked the question, "Dad wants to know how old you are this morning."

Back home, the child reported to his parents, "Mrs. Wells said to tell you to mind your own business."

Why are pianos difficult to get into?
The keys are on the inside.

⊙⊙⊙

A note left for a pianist from his wife: "Gone Chopin, have Liszt, Bach in a minuet."

⊙⊙⊙

Mender's hymn: "Holy, Holy, Holy"
Politician's hymn: "Standing on the Promises"
Shopper's hymn: "In the Sweet By and By"
Shoe repairer's hymn: "It Is Well with My Soul"
Librarian's hymn: "Whispering Hope"
Umpire's hymn: "I Need No Other Argument"
Golfer's hymn: "There Is a Green Hill Far Away"
Haberdasher's hymn: "Blest Be the Tie"
Dot-com sales hymn: "A Charge to Keep I Have"
Gossip's hymn: "Pass It On"

A teenaged couple at a movie theater was more than conspicuous with its audible running commentary about the acting and the plot. At length, a woman seated behind the couple tapped the boy on the shoulder. "Do you want us to ask them to turn down the volume of the movie so you can hear each other more clearly?"

◉⊙◎

On the first day of classes, a brash young college boy asked the pretty girl seated next to him for her phone number.

"It's in the phone book," she told him coyly.

"Under what name?" he pressed.

"That's in the book, too."

◉⊙◎

How do you repair a heartbreak?
With ticker tape.

An accountant is having a hard time sleeping and goes to see his doctor.

"Doctor, I just can't get to sleep at night."

"Have you tried counting sheep?"

"That's the problem. I make a mistake and then spend three hours trying to find it."

◉◉◉

Two rival candidates for a local-government seat happened to meet at a taxi stand. Smith was a wealthy veteran of city hall politics, Brown a middle-income political novice.

"I hate to tell you this, son," said Smith, condescending to offer a bit of frank advice, "but you need money if you ever want to run a successful campaign in this city. *Lots* of money. See this?" He took a wad of bills from a coat pocket. "I always carry plenty of cash and spread it around liberally. For example, when my cabby drops me off, I'll give him a wink, a smile, and a five-dollar bill, and let him know I'm counting on his vote."

Young Brown got to thinking about the tactic and came up with a shoestring-budget variation. When his own cabdriver dropped him off, he quickly stepped out the door without leaving any tip at all. "Be sure to vote for Smith in the city council race next Tuesday!" he called over his shoulder.

◉◉◉

Teacher: "Where is the English Channel?"

Student: "I don't know; we don't get that one on our television."

Why do people with colds feel so tired?
Their noses are running and their fevers are soaring.

◉ ⊙ ◎

The dentist was straightforward with his patient. "Now, this may hurt a bit. We're going to have to give you a shot of local anesthesia."

The patient took the shot in stride, and after the anesthesia had taken effect, the dentist began to drill. Later, job done, he let the patient out of the chair.

The patient turned before leaving and remarked, "Now, this may hurt a bit. I don't have the money to pay. . . ."

◉ ⊙ ◎

Emergency Room receptionist: "What's the problem?"
Incoming patient: "These pains in my sides and back. I feel like I have double pneumonia."
Receptionist: "We have only single beds. Which side would you like to have treated?"

How did Betsy Ross judge her work?
"Sew, sew."

⊙⊙⊙

William: "Did you hear the North and the South are going to refight the Battle of Kennesaw Mountain?"
Wade: "What for?"
William: "Because it wasn't fought on the level the first time."

⊙⊙⊙

How did the Vikings send secret messages?
By Norse code.

What is never requested as a prisoner's last meal?
Minute steak.

⊙⊙⊙

Teacher: "Jeremy, where can we find the Red Sea?"
Jeremy: "Well, there's one at the top of my last test paper."

⊙⊙⊙

Things I Learned in College:

That it didn't matter how late I scheduled my first class—
I'd still sleep through it.

That I could change so much and barely realize it.

That college kids throw airplanes, too.

That if you wear polyester, everyone will ask, "Why are you
so dressed up?"

That every clock on campus shows a different time.

That if you were smart in high school—so what?

That chemistry labs require more time than all my other
classes put together.

That you can know everything and still fail a test.

That you can know nothing and still ace a test.

That most of my education would be obtained outside of my
classes.

That I would be one of those people my parents warned me
about.

That psychology is really biology, biology is really chemistry,
chemistry is really physics, and physics is really math.

That free food served until 10:00 is gone by 9:50—or earlier.

"The prosecutor says she can produce five witnesses who saw you running from the bank with the money bags," a defense lawyer confided to a suspect.

"That's nothing," said the suspect. "I can produce five hundred witnesses who didn't see me running from the bank."

⊙⊙⊚

Judge, to repeat offender: "What are you charged with this time, Mr. Smith?"

Smith: "I was just trying to get my Christmas shopping done early."

Prosecutor: "Yes—before the store opened, Your Honor."

⊙⊙⊚

"It's obvious," said the teacher, "that you haven't studied your geography. What is your excuse?"

"Well," the student replied, "my dad says the world is changing every day, so I thought it would be best if I waited until it settles down."

Knock-knock.
Who's there?
Waddle.
Waddle who?
Waddle you give me if I stop telling these jokes?

⊙⊙⊙

Knock-knock.
Who's there?
Needle.
Needle who?
Needle the help I can get.

⊙⊙⊙

Knock-knock.
Who's there?
Thermos.
Thermos who?
Thermos be someone home; I see a light on.

**Day
358**

A teacher asked the children in her Sunday school class, "If I sold my house and my car, had a big garage sale, and gave all my money to church, would I get to heaven?"

"NO!" the children all answered.

"If I cleaned the church every day, mowed the lawn, and kept everything neat and tidy, would I get to go to heaven?"

Again the answer was "NO!"

"Well," she continued, "then how can I get to heaven?"

In the back of the room, a five-year-old boy shouted, "You gotta be dead!"

◉⊙◎

Why were Adam and Eve considered noisy neighbors?
They raised Cain.

◉⊙◎

The Ten Commandments were the subject of Miss Dixie's Sunday school lesson for five- and six-year-olds. After explaining "Honor thy father and thy mother," Miss Dixie asked, "Is there a commandment that teaches us how to treat our brothers and sisters?"

Without missing a beat, little Cindy answered, "Thou shalt not kill."

What do you call a lemon-eating cat?
A sourpuss.

⊙⊙⊙

What do you get if you cross an alligator with a flower?
I don't know, but I'm not going to smell it!

⊙⊙⊙

A golfing duffer cringed when his drive landed in an anthill. Choosing a sand wedge, he positioned himself and swung at the half-buried ball. Sand and ants flew. The ball hadn't moved.

Again the novice braced and swung. Again the anthill was devastated, but the ball lay unmoved.

Among the panic-stricken ant colony, one ant yelled to his friend, "Come on! That big white ball seems to be a pretty safe place!"

Day
360

"Americans are getting stronger. Twenty years ago it took two people to carry in ten dollars worth of groceries. Today, a five-year-old can do it." —Henny Youngman

◎⊙◎

Bill Vaughn in the *Kansas City Star*: "A real patriot is the fellow who gets a parking ticket and rejoices that the system works."

◎⊙◎

A senior player at the University of Pittsburgh: "I'm going to graduate on time no matter how long it takes."

Coming home from his Little League game, Bud excitedly swung open the front door and hollered, "Anyone home?"

His father immediately asked, "So how did you do, son?"

"You'll never believe it!" Buddy announced. "I was responsible for the winning run!"

"Really? How'd you do that?"

"I dropped the ball."

◉◉◉

"I once lost a wager on a World Wrestling Federation match. My guy was pinned in ten seconds. I couldn't understand it. He'd won the rehearsal."

◉◉◉

Two New York City detectives were investigating the murder of one Juan Flores.

"How was he killed?" asked one detective.

"With a golf gun," the other replied.

"A golf gun? What is a golf gun?"

"I don't know, but it sure made a hole in Juan!"

What force and strength cannot break through,
I with barely a touch can do.
And many in the street would wait,
Were I not a friend to the gate.
What am I?
A key.

⊙⊙⊙

What do you throw out when you need it, but take in when you are done with it?
An anchor.

⊙⊙⊙

A boy was at a carnival and went to a booth where a man said to the boy, "If I write your exact weight on this piece of paper, then you have to give me fifty dollars; but if I can't, I will pay you fifty dollars."

The boy looked around and saw no scale, so he agreed, thinking no matter what the man wrote he'd just say he weighed more or less.

In the end the boy ended up paying the man fifty dollars. How did the man win the bet?
The man did exactly as he said he would and wrote, "Your exact weight," on the paper.

"How's your husband doing with the baby?" a woman asked her friend.

"He's learning. Last night he figured out that you don't wake little Sherie up in order to see her smile."

◉◉◉

"How much money do you think I'm worth, Dad?"

The father regarded his teenaged son thoughtfully.

"To your mother and me, I would say you're priceless."

"Do you think I'm worth a thousand dollars?"

"Certainly."

"A million?"

"Even more than a million, to us."

"Would you mind giving me about twenty of it, then?"

◉◉◉

Robert was explaining to a friend a problem that had arisen in his relationship with Megan. "We have a strong disagreement over our wedding plans," he said.

"She probably wants it to be a big, expensive affair," guessed the friend.

"Not exactly. I keep telling her a small garden wedding would be nice, and she keeps telling me we should start dating other people."

"Always live within your means," a tax consultant advised a client.

"Oh, we do," responded the client. "We just have to take out loans in order to do it."

◉⊙◎

Wife: "Do you love me just because my father left me a fortune?"

Husband: "Not at all, darling. I would love you no matter who left you the money."

◉⊙◎

A man walked into a bank and asked to borrow the sum of two thousand dollars for three weeks. The loan officer asked what collateral the man had. The borrower replied, "I've got a Rolls-Royce. Keep it until the loan is paid off. Here are the keys."

So the loan officer arranged for the car to be driven into the bank's underground parking for safekeeping and gave the borrower two thousand dollars.

Three weeks later, the man walked back into the bank, paid back the two thousand dollar loan plus ten dollars interest, and regained possession of his Rolls-Royce. The loan officer was mystified: "Tell me, sir," he said, "why would someone who drives a Rolls-Royce need to borrow two thousand dollars?"

The borrower smiled and replied, "I had to go abroad for three weeks—where else could I store a Rolls-Royce for that length of time for ten dollars?"

ADD YOUR FAVORITE JOKES HERE

ADD YOUR FAVORITE JOKES HERE

ADD YOUR FAVORITE JOKES HERE

ADD YOUR FAVORITE JOKES HERE

_____

_____

_____

_____

_____

_____

_____

_____

_____

_____

_____

_____

_____

_____

_____

_____

_____

_____

_____

_____

_____

_____

_____

ADD YOUR FAVORITE JOKES HERE

ADD YOUR FAVORITE JOKES HERE

ADD YOUR FAVORITE JOKES HERE

ADD YOUR FAVORITE JOKES HERE

ADD YOUR FAVORITE JOKES HERE

ADD YOUR FAVORITE JOKES HERE

ADD YOUR FAVORITE JOKES HERE

ADD YOUR FAVORITE JOKES HERE

ADD YOUR FAVORITE JOKES HERE